COVERT OPS

To STACY,

You have been an exceptional friend and we have had some great times.

The memories will always be good ones.

SIERRA VISTA, AZ
12 DEC 2015
"GO ARMY"

COVERT OPS

Those were the days my friends ;
The Lives and Times of Covert
US Army CID Agents

BILL IVORY

Rev. date: 09/08/2015

To order additional copies of this book, contact:
Xlibris
1-888-795-4274
www.Xlibris.com
Orders@Xlibris.com
718563

CONTENTS

PROLOGUE

The stories that follow are of real people and real investigations. The stories are true (with just a little embellishment to make them more readable to the public, but not by much. Names have been changed but the persons behind them are very much a part of this history.)

My story begins in the mid-1960s when I joined the US Army CID family. It was an unremarkable beginning for a military policeman who had served as a patrolman at the massive Army Airborne base at Ft Bragg, NC, but what was to follow was a most unique 24 year career which culminated with induction into the prestigious US Army Criminal Investigation Command Hall of fame. The Hall of fame induction ceremony at CID Headquarters at Ft Belvoir, Va was built around the placement of my plaque and photo alongside of so many other CID Agents, the names of whom are firmly implanted in my memory. Each of these men were heroes among CID Agents, having been among those who founded the organization during WW11 and who had been involved in spectacular investigations, both covert, and overt, which had been made the major part of CID's exceptional history. Many of those cases are a history, and a priceless story in and of themselves, from the finding of crown jewels hidden in Nazi treasure troves throughout the world, to major international drug suppression operations. Each of which was expertly handled by CID Agents willing to give all to solve and resolve. They all give testimony to the fantastic training provided to CID as a whole. There were, in fact, CID Agents assigned to the group known As the "Monument Men" who actively sought out stolen works of art,and other valuables stolen by the Nazis during the war. The most prolific thief of them all was Hermann Goering himself who plundered art treasures from France, to what is now Eastern Europe.

The official, and formal Hall of Fame induction ceremony in 2007, was the highlight of the annual CID Ball, held at a major hotel in Springfield, Va. This function, complete with dress blue uniform, and tuxedos for the men, and formal evening dress for the ladies was organized to honor the Agent of the Year, and others who had performed at their best throughout the year, and the placement of the selected CID Special Agents into the hallowed "Hall of Fame". Just to be considered for this great honor is a heart stopping experience for most CID Special Agents. Joining me in this occasion was Special Agent John B. whose career, while different from mine in most ways, was also most impressive.

I was accompanied by my beautiful wife Elisa, who was presented with a beautiful bouquet of flowers which could not match the glow on her face in all of this pomp and circumstance. After the presentation of the Hall of Fame induction to John and myself we were invited to make our acceptance remarks to the Commanding General and all of the dignitaries in attendance. My remarks were built on a desire to impart to all, one of my pet projects which I have attempted to observe during my service with the CID. That is the mentorship of younger and less experienced Agents by those who have been on the business end of the wide variety of criminal investigations throughout the world. The raw talent which is available throughout the ranks of the CID is amazing, and it is virtually untapped.

The Army CID is considered by other investigative agencies of the US Government as being among the top of the line in solving from the simplest to the most intricate of investigations, some of which I will attempt to describe in these pages. It must follow that the memories of these cases could greatly enrich the investigative knowledge of those who have not had the pleasure, or discomfort, of being involved in cases which require daily and in some cases, hourly updates on the cases to the highest level of the US Government.

But, I digress. My remarks dealt with senior Special Agents sharing their "Stuff" with the younger and inexperienced Agents who make up the majority of the CID force. This "Stuff" is that which is not taught in CID school, or other investigative courses. Cannot be found in any books or training films, but is that "Stuff" that is acquired through the school of investigative hard knocks, and is sequestered in the back of the more senior Agents memory banks. I remember being coached thru a variety of cases by these old, salty investigators, some of whom saved my butt with their wisdom. I especially remembered one such "old timer" who had jumped into Normandy the night before D-Day, won the Silver Star and Purple Heart, and was a whiz in solving most cases, and was serving with me in Vietnam awaiting his retirement date. This wizened man, J C, was sharing investigative space with me in one of the many sparcely furnished CID offices found in all of the Vietnam combat zone, and equipped with an old manual typewriter that you had to manually rewind the typing ribbon to get as much mileage out of it as is humanly possible. I was struggling with a rather complex fraud investigation and he saw my pain as I plodded through the boring details of the case. He grabbed me by the scruff of the neck (Literally), and said to me" Bill, Let me show you an easier way to do this." His down home approach to the case made sense, and I have used the same style of approach to many other cases. JC is also the person who saw me struggling with gaining the use of my right arm after being shot in a real estate dispute with members of the Viet Cong in the remote station of Qui Nhon in the northern part of Vietnam. He related how he rehabbed after being severely wounded in a similar real estate dispute, but his was during the battle of the bulge in 1944. I think that there is a physics principal dealing with two objects (or persons) occupying the same space at the same time, which applied to both of our experiences. During the rest of my CID career I tried to emulate JC and I hope those who received my "Stuff" were well served. The people involved in some of the more lucrative frauds, were US Civilians, US military, and Vietnamese civilians who were made millionaires by physically stealing supplies from the docks of the port that serviced Saigon and the whole country, and others who simply turned their heads while the others pilfered war supplies needed by the combat troops. There was one such case that involved Vietnamese civilians that really busted my chops. One of the schemes involved the sale of brass on the international market. The wife of an extremely high ranking Vietnamese General, and another wife of a very high ranking political person ran a black market on stolen US brass that netted multi millions of dollars. The brass was obtained from Vietnamese military artillery units which requisitioned ammunition at a phenomenal rate and then were instructed to aimlessly fire the rounds at nothing in particular in order to collect tons and tons of expended brass artillery shells which were then turned over to a syndicate that sold the brass on the black market as far away as Hong Kong. I clearly remember hearing the all night firing sessions of the Vietnamese army units. One was located next to a US base on which I spent a lot of time. and I blame that firing on my severe hearing loss I experienced as a result of my wartime service. A good friend of mine who was also assigned to the Logistical Crime Suppression Team as a senior CID Agent got involved in a particularly dangerous aspect of this scheme when he discovered that a Korean ship was about to sail from a Vietnamese port carrying stolen US tactical vehicles, and a large supply of the expended brass. When he confronted the ship's captain, and told him the ship was not going to sail with the illicit cargo, the Korean captain had Korean soldiers he was also transporting, draw their firearms and protect the criminal operation. This toe to toe confrontational situation turned into a diplomatic headache for the US Embassy since one of the stolen Jeeps on board was destined for the personal use of a high ranking Korean officer once it reached Korea. My friend was told to stand down and not interfere with the ship leaving, and that a token of a very minor portion of the cargo would be left at the port. It was learned that the US Ambassador was personally involved with that decision. The General's wives were spared the loss of the brass and vehicles by a very high level and corrupt Vietnamese official. This was but one of the multitude of illegal schemes uncovered by CID that was covered up by officials.

My remarks at the Hall of Fame ceremony reached home with a lot of the attendees, and after the ceremonies were over, many of them from Sergeants through General approached me and expressed their hopes to be mentored by some more experienced investigators. I continue to do this to this day, and hopefully I will make a difference with some of the Agents. My memories of this day continue to amaze me. That I was considered qualified to stand next to the others in the Hall of Fame, both humbled me and made me proud to be a part of this great assembly of great men.

My uniformed experience as a patrolman, and a highway patrolman on the Autobahns of Germany are what led me to prepare an application to the Provost Marshal General, Carl C. This was during my tour of duty in rural France after leaving a year of life in Seoul, Korea as the driver and bodyguard for a full Colonel who was the 8th US Army Provost Marshal. During this tour of duty I accompanied the Provost Marshal, known as "Gus" to a remote Turkish Army base in the northern portion of South Korea where a unit of the Turkish army had caught three South Koreans who had been stealing from the Turkish soldiers' barracks. They were going to serve summary justice on the Koreans, and as Chief of Police for all of the UN Troops in Korea, Gus was going to try to be the peacemaker and resolve this situation. By the time we made it to the Turkish camp, the justice had already been administered. The Turkish troops had taken the cleaning rods they used to clean their rifles, and hammered them through the ear canals of the thiefs, and had strung them up, and were going to leave them hanging there as a lesson to all who would steal from them. Gus, the ultimate politician, immediately got next to the Turkish Colonel who commanded the Turkish troops, and convinced him to have the three dead Koreans removed from the trees they were hanging from. When this was done, we drove back to Seoul, pleased that the Turks didn't turn on us. When things in Seoul were quiet, which wasn't very often, Old "Gus" had me reading CID cases and prompted me to apply for my CID Badge and credentials which I did in 1964 while stationed at Trois Fontaines, France, the largest ammunition storage depot in Europe. After being accepted as a probie Agent, I stayed on during the phase out of all US military activities in France after the President, Gen Charles DeGaulle, demanded that we leave.

THE KHAKI MAFIA

꩜ ⊙꙼

My exposure to major cases started in France. One in particular was made a part of a major novel in which the Sergeant Major of the Army was convicted and jailed for his part in the extortion and larceny of millions of dollars from the network of Non-Commissioned Officer (NCO) clubs which were and still are a major part of military life on installations all over the world. Some of the more senior NCOs systematically, looted the clubs of funds collected in the slot machines by either blocking mechanisms designed to count machine plays and then skimming off countless funds at the end of each night, and also by preparing false jackpot payout sheets and pocketing the proceeds which ran from $500.00 to $1,000.00 each which were then funneled into the accounts of those involved. . I spent many a day and some long nights going through boxes of jackpot payout sheets and doing a field comparison of handwriting and signatures on them before sending them to the Criminal Investigations Laboratory in Frankfurt, Germany, and then interviewing those whose names appeared as winners. It was tedious work, but when I saw that it made a difference, it made it all worthwhile. This conspiracy was one built by the senior Non–Commissioned Officers stationed throughout the world including the United States, Vietnam, Korea and other locations, wherever slot machines and floor shows existed. Kickbacks from the entertainers also came into play. That, and other cases from simple larcenies to death investigations rounded off my initial investigative assignment, and somewhat prepared me for what was to come. Special Agent Hugh H. was the Special Agent in Charge of the Trois Fontaines CID office, and his expertise in interviewing and interrogations was not lost on me. His techniques stood me well in years to come, and his method of plodding through paperwork made me a hero of sorts when I found a huge bunker full of ammunition and explosives which had been reported stolen from the largest ammo depot in Europe. I guess that must have made an impression on the big boss who was stationed in faraway Orleans, France. When Hugh left France on rotation to the US, the boss, LTC Ferdinand "The Bull" left me in Charge of the Trois Fontaines office until it finally closed. While waiting for this magic date to come, I became involved in a monstrous larceny case which involved three other installations which were also in my area of jurisdiction. There were a number of large warehouses that contained enough medical equipment to build several well equipped field hospitals In the event the "Cold war" heated up, and casualties began to flow. Each warehouse was stacked from ground level, to 30 or more feet high with the medical equipment. The buildings themselves were 50 to 100 yards long and about 40 yards wide. I never learned the value of all of the equipment but it had to be in the multi-millions of dollars.

Each building was guarded by a Labor Service Company manned by refugees from communist Poland. The commander of these security forces was a Labor Service Major. Each building and its contents were supposed to be inventoried every quarter by the Labor Service Commander and his staff. Each inventory report was neatly filed when there were no discrepancies noted. Occasionally, the American commander of the US Army Medical Depot would make an inspection, and his report was also neatly filed. When the news of the departure of all US Forces and equipment from France was received, there was widespread panic throughout what was called the NATO Communications Zone. Nothing was ever supposed to be moved from here. There were suicides and desertions throughout France. When movers came to empty the buildings of the medical equipment, they found that the huge stacks of crates from floor to ceiling were hollow. Each one had been systematically emptied by what had to be a very organized crime group. But how could this happen with armed guards on the buildings 24/7? What few CID Agents remained in France at that time were rounded up and under the leadership of LTC "Sully" de Fontaines who is famous, or infamous for his exploits while serving as an officer in the US Army Special Forces, we began an investigation which implicated people who had been stationed there as US Army or Polish Labor service personnel for 20 or more years. The Polish Major disappeared back into Poland, and all of the lower ranking persons were scooped up by the French Customs Police. It was a miracle we didn't need the equipment. It would have taken more than a year to replace it, if at all. The French courts did not find this case amusing. There was a lot of jail time handed out, and there was a lot of money that changed hands over the years, and the French Customs Police wanted their share. A lot of the equipment had been shipped to other countries, some of which were not friendly to the US, and disposed of on the black market. I met with an inspector of the French Customs Police, who I had known for years, many months later, and we talked about the case. It seemed that of the higher-ups in this case, most disappeared before going to trial, and it was the little guys who took the big fall.

My next assignment in CID was to the Bamberg, Germany office. Here I found myself in the middle of a hard working police operation that exposed me to the nuts and bolts of the CID Program; drugs and death.

Author as 508th MP Bn, Military Policeman in Germany in 1962

NUTS AND BOLTS

It was here that I found another "Old Timer" who was willing to help a struggling newby with his vast experience. Lester L was another WW11 Agent who fought his way across Europe, and then joined the CID. He was of all things, a trained hangman who was active during the Nuernberg War Crimes Trial. No stranger to death, he was extremely methodical in his approach to death investigations. One murder he brought me in on was that of a soldier thought to be AWOL or a deserter, whose corpse was found floating in the river that flowed through Bamberg. A thick belt had been fastened around the chest area and he had been beaten before being thrown in the river to drown. The rest of his appearance indicated that he was a US soldier. Lester mobilized some of his collection of informants, and learned that the body was indeed that of a missing soldier, and the belt around his chest was the trademark of a band of gypsy drug dealers working the Bamberg area. Lester's fluency in German was invaluable when dealing with the German criminal Police (The KRIPO).

The info developed by us assisted the German Police in identifying the perpetrators who had an INTERPOL warrant drawn for their arrest. The investigation was not without a hiccup though. The body, when pulled from the river, was taken to the US Army medical facility on one of the installations in the historic city. We photographed the body in the state that we found it and were told by the KRIPO not to touch the body before a German medical examiner could see it. We were to leave it exactly as it was, laying in the US medical facility with the belt fastened around the chest. We were ready to comply until the time that the body, having come from the cold river, began to heat up, smell, and also to begin swelling. This combination made it obvious to all there that something unpleasant was about to happen. The attending US physician stated the obvious when he said that if we didn't do something the body was going to explode. A call to the KRIPO advised that the medical examiner, who was in far away Wuerzburg was at least two hours out of Bamberg, and that he was adamant that the body and all on it not be touched. We took it for about another hour when the stench was approaching being intolerant, when Lester in his infinite wisdom said "screw this" produced an illegal switchblade and began to cut through the belt. Thus relieved from exploding, the body was wheeled outside in a large empty parking lot to await the arrival of the Germans medical personnel who, when they saw what had happened, were speechless. The KRIPO were sympathetic, and they promised to sooth the feelings of the medical team, which they did. The US medical facility however didn't fare so well. They had to repaint the entire place in an attempt to get rid of the death stench. The only regret I have from this assignment is while he shared a lot of investigative "Stuff" with me he carefully avoided speaking about his hangman's time. He did tell me one time while we were enjoying a happy hour at the Officer's Club, that that was private time between himself and those he had to deal with.

DUTY AGENT

Introduction to the life of a "Duty Agent" is something that all Agents have to participate in. Being the representative of the CID is a sacred trust which must be followed and experienced with great care and tact. Dealing with the public after hours is an adventure which some Agents dislike and others can't get enough of. Bamberg was no different than any other place I was assigned. Calls about robberies, rapes, assaults, and much more are frequently the cause of lack of sleep for the duty Agent. While handling one complaint of rape from a walk-in to the MP Desk, the so called victim told me that she had met a GI at a small club in Old town Bamberg and had taken him to her apartment for a little romp. Before they jumped into the sack, she told him how much it would cost. He agreed and they had their fun, and then the GI told her he had to go, and he got dressed, and as he was leaving the apartment he reached over to the bedside table and retrieved the cash he had given her. She objected loudly but he kept going. Unfortunately for him he was wearing his duty uniform which had his name tag on it. She remembered the name and gave it to me. I recognized the name as one of the local Engineer Battalion's First Sergeants. This was not going to be a good night for him. She also told me that while they were making love he bit her on her not so private female part. She then pulled up her skirt and was trying to show me the mark he had left. I told her to stop and called for the MP Desk Sergeant who also worked in the same building. When he arrived I explained the law to her about rape and also larceny. I could call the man in and investigate him for stealing the money, but would have to report the alleged rape to the German police. This stopped her cold. She knew how the German police dealt with prostitutes, and she suddenly withdrew her complaint, and left. The desk sergeant and I had a little chuckle over it, and then I had him send a patrol over to the senior NCO quarters and bring the First Sergeant back to see me. What he said he wanted to do was go and get the female and bring her back. He told me that he would have no problem looking at her injury. When the First Sergeant arrived I ate his ass for being such a jerk. He was very humble, and apologetic and begged me not to report him to his organization. He knew that the Battalion Commander would skin him alive if he knew. There are times when common sense must take hold, and a little sympathy shown, especially when the First Sergeant ran a company that had most of the criminals we dealt with assigned to it. To have him on our side, owing us a favor or two, would not hurt. He repaid us many times over.

One of the chores I had while on duty was to observe activities at the "Lower 4 Club" which is the place that privates and those not NCOs yet can congregate and relax after a hard day fighting the Cold War. The Lower 4 club is also known at the place to go if you are aching for a fist fight or needed a little marijuana The MPs are kept busy keeping the peace. Sometimes they are even successful. But not often enough. Weekends the club is like a war zone. Often, as I drove around the installation, I would cruise by the Club to see what was going on, especially when the MPs were dispatched there on a fight call. On one fateful night while driving near the club I monitored a call of a fight in the parking lot. I rolled into an area and parked away from the action and watched as the two MPs who responded handcuffed a soldier, and then they lost control. Instead of placing him in their patrol vehicle, they, for some unknown reason, took him back into the club. A very bad idea. I got out of my vehicle and approached the club. Being in civilian clothes permitted me to walk thru a mounting crowd to the club. I entered, and saw the MPs and their prisoner by the dance floor. The club manager, an extremely large man was also there. I went to him and told him we had to get the MPs out of there before we had a very bad incident. He agreed and he approached one of the MPs and told him of the approaching disaster. The MPs then started escorting their prisoner back towards the exit. Soldiers, in the best of times don't like MPs, and dislike even more when one of theirs is being handcuffed and hauled away. They were vocalizing their feelings when one of then threw a trash can at the MPs, knocking one of them down. Sensing the blood in the air the crowd of at least 50, which had exited the club behind the MPs, began their attack. The MP vehicle was about 15-20 yards away and the crowd had effectively separated the two MPs, one of whom had regained his feet and had drawn his nightstick to protect himself. Seeing that the crowd was about to overwhelm the MP, and mindful that they had loaded sidearms on them, I decided to take some part in extricating them from this mob. . To the rear of them I saw the club manager and signaled him to assist me in getting to the MP vehicle. He complied and together we forced our way to the MP Jeep. I climbed on the hood of the Jeep where I could see the MPs being beaten by the mob. I pulled my weapon which was a 2 inch barrel colt .38 special that had a 5 round load. As the overwhelmed MPs were trying to get away from the mob, I saw another crowd of soldiers exiting the club and trying to enter the fray. I fired one round in the air in the direction of the huge parade field to distract and hopefully scare them off. By doing this I became the new target and three men tried to mount the jeep hood with what looked like 2X4s. I let another round off hitting one of them, and that caused them all to disperse. One of the MPs said that his weapon was gone and that told me that we were in deep kimchi and had to do something quickly. The club manager had reentered the club and called the MPs telling them what was happening. The Desk Sgt then dispatched all units to the club. I grabbed the more injured of the two MPs and started towards my unmarked car, telling the other MP to head for it as well. As I did this another man from the club mob approached with a 2X4 and I took aim at his head and was about to blow it away when he saw that I was serious and dropped the club and disappeared into the night. About this time patrols began to arrive from other installations around Bamberg running code 3. I then gave the injured MP to a Sgt and headed back to the club, looking for the manager. I found him on the ground by the club entrance and as he straightened up he was holding the MPs .45 pistol which he had seen laying on the ground. The other Agents from the CID Office also appeared on scene having been called by the MP Desk Sgt. When all was sorted out we learned that the 2X4s had been taken from a stack of lumber by a construction site nearby, and the soldiers ended up beating each other with them after the attack on the MPs started. The MPs learned a bitter lesson that night. Once you have your target handcuffed, get out of the area immediately and don't reenter the place where the incident all started. The man shot off of the Jeep hood survived with a round in his thigh.

The next step in my indoctrination as a CID Agent was a sign of bigger things to come.

DRUGS & INTRIGUE

Germany, at that time in history, was ripe with drug dealing and prolific drug use by US military personnel. The CID Headquarters in Heidelberg had years earlier instituted a covert Narcotics Suppression Team made up of experienced CID Special Agents and an army of paid informants. All, with false names and identity papers were assigned to work with European Narcotics Offices in Germany, Italy, and Holland using informants and undercover Agents to identify and make major purchases of large quantities of all sorts of illegal drugs from the dealers, and assist in the apprehension of the dealers. Funded by a special contingency fund, the undercover operation was extremely successful. Among the Agents assigned to this group was one notorious Agent called "ACE". His successes in this newly developing CID specialty field were and still are impressive and infamous, and more than qualified him for his position within the CID Hall of Fame, where his plaque and photo are enshrined. The tactics used were somewhat questionable, but their obvious successes more than made up for them. Well, not always. There was this one time when one of the more experienced Agents, lets call him Del, bought what was purported to be 5 kilos of heroin, which in fact was kitty litter. He is still razzed about that caper.

I first met "ACE" at the covert headquarters of the Narcotics team which was in Mannheim, Germany. He knew I was assigned to the Bamberg Office, and he approached me and asked me if I would be interested in assisting him in a drug investigation in the Nuernberg area. He wanted me since I still looked like a typical GI, which was what he needed for this job. The plan was for me to join with a soldier informant, who had also been arrested for dealing Hashish, and be introduced as another dealer looking for a drug source. Ace wanted me to make 3 separate buys from the Turkish dealer, and then the German Police would raid his house and arrest everyone in it and seize all drugs which they would find in the house. The Germans wanted an Agent, rather than an informant, to make the three mandatory buys on the Turk before they busted him. It sounded interesting, and I wanted to try it but I told Ace that I had to ask the Bamberg boss for permission. He said that would not be a problem since he had already told him he wanted me. The next day I travelled to Nuernberg and at a remote location (read Safe House) I met with the Germans and we went through the operational plans. Everything seemed OK so we proceeded to another location where I met with the informant where he was searched to make sure he wasn't carrying anything, neither drugs nor weapons. We then went in the informant's car to the neighborhood of the drug dealer. We agreed that he would introduce me as a dealer from a training area about 3 hours' drive from Nuernberg and that I was looking for a long term supplier of hashish for me to take back with me to the training area. We parked and walked a short distance to a very crowded neighborhood where he pointed out the location of his dealer contact. We entered the house after a very close scrutiny by a man, about 30 yrs old, who answered the door. We were apparently accepted since an older man in the house came and greeted the informant like an old friend. Once inside I was searched for a wire, or weapons and we then sat on a couch across from the older man. Using the informant as a translator using pigeon English and some German words we established that I was in the market for hashish. I would like to make a small purchase of his wares to test the potency and then more to establish myself with the drug users in the training area. The older man agreed that we could do business but it had to be his way. I initially purchased about 1½ kilos of hashish, and the old man said now I had to smoke some with him. I argued that I had to drive 3 hours back to my training area and didn't want to wreck my car. He agreed and I left with the informant and the purchased drugs. On the drive back to the location where Ace was waiting, the informant told me that he had also made a purchase of a few small pieces of hash for his personal consumption. When we met with Ace and his team, I gave him the 1 ½ kilo I had purchased and on the side told him of the informants purchase. He then searched the informant and took the pieces from him. This really pissed off the informant but he knew better than to let Ace know it. He was facing about 5 years for trafficking so he felt that giving up the dope was in a good cause.

We did the same a few nights later and all went well. The third time I was looking for a couple of kilo blocks that I was supposed to sell to incoming trainees. The deal went as the others until the old man said that this time I had to smoke some before I left the house. I argued again on the same premise, that

I didn't want to kill myself in a car wreck. The old man then pulled from a nearby table a very long kitchen carving knife that looked to me at the time to be a sword. He placed the knife at my throat and said "Smoke or die". I had previously discussed this with Ace and he said that if I couldn't fake it, to try to take small pulls on the pipe. Knowing that this was legal to do it this way according to existing regulations I settled down for the deal. Plans also called for me to be wired since I hadn't been searched the second visit. When I gave a coded signal the police would make their entry and make the bust. I took the pipe and took real small pulls on it and made the old man happy, since he knew that the German Police were prohibited from smoking during a deal. As I started to exit the house with the 2 blocks of hash in a plastic bag, I gave the signal, and nothing happened. I gave it again, and again but nothing happened. I finally said loudly, "where in the hell are you guys", and still nothing happened. By the time I reached the car I was the one who was pissed, and also feeling the effects of the hash. When I reached Ace at the meeting place he was all apologetic, but stated that at the last minute the Germans said they were changing the plan. I gave him the two kilos of hash and then met with an MI Agent who I knew from Bamberg for the ride back. He had his wife riding in the front passenger seat of the car. As we rode home I had the sudden urge to reach around and grab her by the throat and choke her. I told this to my friend who thought I was joking, but I wasn't. This was a part of the after action report made on the deal. The reason the Germans cancelled the bust was never made clear, but they offered that there was a new strain of hashish on the streets that caused hallucinations. (and I had to be the one to verify this for them.) They finally raided the Turk's house after a few days and found more drugs and made the arrest. I told Ace that I didn't think I wanted to work with those German police again. He agreed.

After that adventure, it was back to the office routine of the Bamberg CID. Duty Agent calls, report writing, and other chores which keep the everyday lives of CID Agents full of things to keep them busy. One such call was of an explosion at an off post home of two soldiers. The explosion caused severe injuries to two of the persons living there which caused them to be medically evacuated to Torrejon Air Force Base in Spain, and finally to the burn center at San Antonio, Texas. Investigations must continue, and, Investigative leads were prepared and sent to the Office of Special Investigations at the nearby Air Force Base in Spain, and CID at San Antonio, Questions were prepared so that the Investigators could more easily obtain the needed information. It was determined that the soldiers living in that house had stolen explosives during a training exercise and were experimenting with then just prior to them exploding. The uninjured soldiers were arrested and tried in a General Courts Martial for their part in the senseless incident. Another call was to initiate a search and rescue operation to locate a local Battalion Commander's aircraft which had been missing for several hours. Why CID? Well CID investigates all non-combat and unattended deaths of military personnel within its jurisdictional area. We found the commander, but not in time. He had perished in the aircraft crash. My year's time in Bamberg was somewhat short owing to the other overseas time spent in France. Off I was again and this time it was a return trip to the sprawling base at Fort Bragg, NC. A return home so to speak, for this is where I began my police career.

Ft Bragg, NC is at the best of times a very busy installation. One of the largest in the United States, it is home to the elite Special Forces, and the 82d Airborne Division. When I arrived in 1968 it was not in the best of times. A huge US Army Basic Training operation was in full swing. The war in Vietnam was in full swing, and the 1968 Tet Offensive was still on the minds of everyone. Not to be outdone by those memories, the basic training soldiers were busy learning to march, shoot, salute and find ways to avoid service in the war zone. Local communities were experiencing demonstrations against the war and Fayetteville, or Fayettenam as it was lovingly known by the troops, was not immune. Celebrities were more often than not, also seen in the midst of many demonstrations throughout the country. One such famous female Hollywood movie star and known opponent of the war, and supporter of the enemy made it known that she would be joining a demonstration within the Army Basic Training area of Ft Bragg, and was inciting trainees to desert the military in an effort to derail the Vietnam replacement efforts. Ft Bragg, at that time, was an "Open" Post. That is, there were no gate guards to deny the demonstrators entrance to the post. Taking advantage of this, the demonstrators flooded into the Basic Training area, and immediately started to get rowdy, ignoring the orders of the Commanding General, and of course everyone's favorite movie star was right in the forefront of all of this calling for the soldiers to leave the installation, and go home. The CID office was also represented in all of this, observing and noting those who were ringleaders in the event of further trouble. The most active of the CID Agents were from the local drug suppression task force, who, in their normal work garb were indistinguishable from other demonstrators from the off post hippie type community. The movie star was the most vocal of all and when ordered by the General to cease and desist, she came out with a string of cuss phrases that would have made a longshoremen's union meeting proud. That someone's mother would allow such activity is extremely doubtful. This unladylike demonstration of the misuse of the English language tipped the scales, and when she continued to rant and rave about the troops deserting immediately, the General ordered her arrest. Accompanying some of the drug task force, agents from the Bragg CID office we placed her in handcuffs over her strong vocal objections which was worse than her demonstration earlier, and she was unceremoniously tossed in the back seat of my CID car, and taken to the MP Station and further to the US magistrate in Fayetteville, where she appeared before him and was released. Inciting the troops to desert charges against her were subsequently dropped. So much for even handed justice.

The troops, caught up in her rhetoric, continued to attempt to avoid combat duty, even after all of the demonstrators had been escorted off post that day. They began to inflict injuries to themselves, engage in drug possession and abuse, committed crimes, such as robbery, assault and refusing to obey their chain of command, all in hope of being dishonorably discharged from the service. This of course was long before the " "Don't Ask, Don't Tell" era, and many of the troops, following the advice of the local shit house lawyers, began to make the pilgrimage to the CID office to confess that they were homosexual, and should be eliminated from the Army. Part of this advice they received through the grapevine, included that they if asked with whom they had performed the homosexual act they should name some Hollywood movie star who they heard would never be contacted to verify the sexual contact. CID Duty Agents were overwhelmed with such reports almost daily, until one of the Agents, interviewing one such confessor, brought him into the busy main admin section of the office to be interviewed and proclaimed loudly to the subject that it was so loud there he had to speak up in order to be heard. The specific questions asked would make most listeners blush, and the subject's answers were then repeated back to him, also very loudly. Often, bystanders would stop and listen to the interviews. The subject would then withdraw his admission of sodomy, and returned to his unit, never to be seen in the CID office again. This tactic caught on in the office. The soldier's grapevine also picked up on this and the flow began to ebb, and finally disappeared. One of these self-admitted violators was encountered in the men's room of a local bar dressed in a lovely short skirt and a cute blouse he was wearing which he had stuffed with a padded bra. Apparently some of the other male patrons of the bar objected to this display and called the local police who promptly arrested him. The airborne paratrooper from the elite 82d Airborne Division was turned over to the MPs who were more than happy to turn him over to me. Since he was an NCO I *called his commanding officer, a Captain, who arrived at the CID office demanding to know why one of his finest troopers was being held. I showed him polaroid photos that had been taken of him as he undressed in the MP station. The Captain became very meek, and ordered the paratrooper to jog back to the Company area along side of his private car. I was told the next day that the Sergeant was paraded through the company area in his costume to the amusement of the rest of the company's men.*

The 6th of April of 1968 was a quiet day at the Ft Bragg CID office. Routine calls, minor crimes, nothing to write home about.

That is until the news broke that someone had killed Martin Luther King in Atlanta by shooting him at the motel where he was staying. What really upset the quiet spring day in North Carolina was that the 82d Airborne Division which is stationed at Ft Bragg was alerted to deploy to Washington, DC to assist the Washington, DC Police Department in quelling the extensive rioting which was occurring. Huge mobs of African Americans were forming, breaking into stores in the shopping districts, and looting the goods. What business was this of the Army you ask?? The Commander in Chief had been advised, based on the widespread violence, to nationalize the 82d ABN Div which had been trained in riot control, and have them immediately transported by the fastest means available to Washington, DC to bring a halt to the rioting which by that time had also included the widespread burning of residential neighborhoods in the north-west district of the Capitol. To fully support the 82d Abn Division, the 503rd Military Police Battalion, which was also stationed at Ft Bragg, was one of the premier riot control units the Army had. It was also alerted and joined the division at the adjoining Pope Air Force Base where we loaded onto C-130s for the flight to Washington.

It was a one hour flight to Washington, DC, and the 82d was immediately sent to secure the many federal buildings including the White House from the rioters. The fires which had been started could easily be seen from the north side of the White House. Both residential and commercial buildings had been targeted by the time we arrived, and the streets were filled with out of control rioters. The situation was getting desperate for the DC Police. The 503d MP Bn was shuttled from the airport to the Potomac Park area of DC where we set up a tent city which was to be our home for the duration. But before settling down for the night, an overview briefing was presented by a representative of the Pentagon. The Bn was briefed on the situation and then assignments were made, and the various sections and companies were assigned different section of DC to begin patrolling alongside the DC police. The CID cell which consisted of 4 Special agents was assigned to ride with members of the DC Police in their patrol vehicles and we were instructed to assist them whenever possible. Prior to departing from Ft Bragg I managed to exchange my cal .38 snub-nosed pistol for the more formidable M1911A1 Cal .45 pistol which felt very reassuring. The DC unit to which I was assigned was to roam around part of the North-west district, observing the rioting mobs, and reporting their locations and direction of travel. The mobs were converging on the businesses in the district and after looting them of everything portable they were burning the buildings. There was no rhyme or reason to their activities, they were just in a free shopping mode. To further illustrate this, many of the buildings being burned housed the very people who were burning them. This we learned as we arrested some of the rioters who readily admitted it. There was no focal point for the riots, or rioters, no demands for justice by them, it was just a bloodlust for destruction, and theft of the wide variety of goods to be found in the upscale stores and mom and pop shops alike. Liquor stores were among the first of the small shops to experience the mindless rioting. It became commonplace to see a looter with a TV on one shoulder and a case of beer or some other liquor on the other To properly set the stage for our activities, it might be helpful to know that the 503d MP Bn was a Combat Military Police unit which was equipped for all out war. We looked just like the 82d Abn Div troops we were there to support. One piece of equipment each of us had was a bulletproof FLAK Jacket. The DC police had no armor at all for their patrolmen. They were more than envious of us over this and they begged us to get some for them. This was more than called for since in many of the districts we entered, we encountered erratic sniper fire which hit several of the officers. Being senior NCOs and Warrant Officers, many of whom were Vietnam War Vets, well versed in the art of scrounging to build office space to conduct investigations in a war zone, we somehow collected a number of serviceable FLAK jackets from the Battalion HQ, and also sent a request to our Ft Bragg office for more. When we started to give them to the extremely grateful DC officers we were working with, we were offered a lot of money for them which we of course refused. During one patrol shift, the unit I was assigned to was ordered to monitor a large gang of rioters which was moving towards the prominent Dupont Circle. Other units were to join with us and attempt to corral the rioters there. As the looters entered the large circle, a large number of them broke off and eventually entered an underground parking garage. Being mindful that there were a lot of expensive automobiles parked in the garage something had to be done before the mob destroyed some, or all of the parked vehicles. A tactical unit arrived on scene and immediately began to issue teargas grenades to all units there. On order, we pulled the grenade pins and rolled the grenades down into the garage. The effect was instantaneous. The rioters came out of the garage at a full run as if they were on fire. The rest of that shift was relatively quiet after that. We remained in our tent city in the beautiful Potomac Park through the Cherry blossom festival and past the 4th of July. While walking through the blossoming cherry trees, quite a few of the lovely DC ladies would stop and engage the resting MPs in conversation. There were a number of relationships started there that would make interesting stories all on their own. The riots thankfully ran out of steam, but not before destroying entire neighborhoods. And suddenly, just like someone said the fun and games are over, it became quiet again. There were no parades when we returned, we just picked up where we left off.

The crimes in and around the Basic Trainees continued with numerous complaints of rape and assault becoming so bad that CID Agents began patrolling the installation at night trying to catch the perps red handed. Some of the targets of these acts were wives of trainees walking alone on post near hotel like guest houses where they stayed on weekends while visiting their husbands. A number of them were accosted as they entered the guest house and forced into their rented rooms, and then sexually attacked.

Each of the guest houses had a resident manager who lived in the hotel to insure that only authorized persons entered the building. When called, the MPs who were patrolling nearby were quick to respond, and take direct and violent action when they encountered and apprehended the trespassers. One night, while Duty Agent, I was called by one of the resident managers who asked me to come by and assist her with a problem. When I arrived, she took me to the furnace room of the World War 11 era wooden building and showed me a spot on the wall of the room where there was a series of holes drilled in the wooden wall which gave visual access to the next room which was the ladies shower and bathroom. In looking through the holes it was obvious that someone had drilled the holes in strategic places in order to observe the ladies bathing, and it was obvious that the person, or persons had been using the location for an extended period.

The next day at the office business meeting which occurred each morning for all Agents to hear what had occurred the previous duty day, I briefed what I had found to the group, and was happily surprised to see that this disturbed the Agents very much that someone would do this to the young ladies staying at the Guest house. They also knew that this could be a preliminary act to someone gaining entry to the building and attacking one or more of the bathers.

Our office was lucky in that we had a number of former Special Forces soldiers who had crossed over into the CID program after having been wounded in Vietnam and unable to continue in combat as an operator. Everyone of them immediately volunteered to form an apprehension team and rid the installation of the perverts who were using this furnace room for their weird pleasures. A surveillance operation was planned for the following weekend when the most visitors would be staying at the Guest House. The planners; our former Special Forces troops of course. Some of the Special Forces Agents had been involved in supporting Operation Phoenix in Vietnam where they had snatched Viet Cong leaders using their commando tactics. The plan which they developed would have made any Special Forces Commander proud. When Friday evening rolled around the entire office was there to support in some way the activity which was about to unfold. As soon as darkness fell, the former commandos melted into the surrounding area, part of which was a wooded area. As case officer, I was right there with them. We were all dressed in camouflaged combat uniforms, and armed to the teeth. I personally had a 12 gauge shotgun loaded with alternating 00 buckshot and slugs. There was no way whoever was using that furnace room was going to get away. Two of the team low crawled, under cover of darkness, underneath the building which had a crawl space about two feet high under the entire building. They would hear if anyone entered the furnace room, and notify the other team members who would silently approach the building, enter and make the arrest. We stayed laid in until about 10:30 PM when one of the close-in team broke squelch on his radio, signaling that someone was in the furnace room. According to the plan, we would all wait until the creeps in the room had settled down. One reason was to give the person(s) in the room time to reach through one of the holes and physically move a loose sheet of metal which had been placed covering the drilled holes in the wall. One of the volunteers from the office was a female who would enter the bathroom with a towel and toilet kit as if she were to take a bath, thereby giving us an overt act by the peepers which was insisted upon by the local JAG prosecutors. During this interval the rest of the arrest team silently made their way to the furnace room door, and when the signal was given that the metal sheet had been moved, we burst into the room. Illuminated it with large spotlights we carried and caught them red handed. Unfortunately for one of them, the shock of seeing the camouflaged warriors descend on them with shotguns at the ready with a round of ammo being racked into the chamber caused him to drop a very smelly load in his pants.

Back at the office, once cleaned up, (hosed down in the parking lot) they were both interrogated and confessed to have been using the furnace room for months. One was a soldier stationed at Ft Bragg, the other was a civilian friend of his who had tagged along with him. The soldier was court martialed and placed in the post stockade. The civilian was turned over to the FBI, who charged him with illegal entry onto a military post with intent to commit a crime.

The manager of the guest house was happy and quite relieved to see this come to an end. This was not the last time we would use the expertise of our Special Forces brothers.

In a similar, but completely separate investigation, there was a rash of rapes in government quarters which was occurring to wives whose husbands were from the same command. They were being attacked in their houses in the early hours of the morning, often around 4;00 or 5 AM, shortly after the husbands left the house for work or when the unit was leaving their barracks area for some type of field duty The entry would be made into the house through a knock on the door and when opened, a home invasion would occur. The man would then attack the wife sexually and leave quickly, usually within a very few minutes. He was always armed with a Kabar knife. When he spoke to the women he was always apologetic about his actions, and none of the victims were physically harmed. these depraved acts of violence also incensed the former SF Agents, and when asked for volunteers to set up a sting, there was no shortage of upraised hands. The sting plan, while risky, came together like this. We knew that the assaults were taking place in a certain area of the post, and that helped in the planning. Also on the installation, was what was known as the WAC Detachment, or a unit 100% composed of women. This of course was in that era of women being segregated from the male population in their living quarters. The First Sergeant of that Wac Detachment, who also worked in the post hospital was a friend of the CID, having assisted us in numerous cases. She was asked to approach some of her female soldiers and after swearing them to complete secrecy, ask them if they would volunteer for a long term dangerous assignment with the CID which could involve some violence, but not on their part. The first Sergeant was also asked to pick some attractive females for this job. (how Sexist!!) She agreed and went at it with great speed, and enthusiasm. She selected 10 attractive ladies of which we selected 5 for the operation from those who volunteered, and they were briefed on the case. The plan was to select quarters in the area of the assaults and plant the females in some unoccupied quarters that had furnishings in them, and have the females act as if they were alone in the quarters. As evenings wore on they would walk through the quarters dressed provocatively, some of the times in revealing night gowns, and leave their drapes open, and house lights on. This was to occur both late at night and also early in the morning. Part of the attackers Method of Operation (MO) was to scout out the area in the housing area, at times even approaching the buildings and peeking through the windows. This was bourne out by the crime scene processing of those quarters which had been invaded by this rapist. There were similar footprints, later positively identified by the CID Crime Lab, by the windows of several of the quarters that had been invaded. The planning was for an extended period of time since we didn't know when, or where, the attacker would next show himself. Of course we could not leave these lovely ladies alone and unprotected in this situation, instead we left each of them with 4 CID Agents, who were again heavily armed, hidden in a part of the house where they could observe what was happening in the quarters, and respond instantly if needed, but not visible to anyone outside.

Our former SF guys were split between duty inside the quarters, and some who would lay in within the treeline that surrounded most of the neighborhoods. During the operation, these teams occasionally switched responsibility, and duty locations.

One thing that was a constant among the SF troops was that they, who had often deployed to Vietnam, were very protective of wives left behind at the mercy of assholes like the villain we were trying to catch. There was always talk before going on stake-out about what would be justice for this guy.

It turned out to be an extended mission since our perp wasn't active for about a month. But, in that month our WAC partners were superb in acting out their parts, some even made a game out of it, and drove our inside the quarters stake out teams crazy with their antics, especially when wearing their sexy outfits we bought for them using government funds. One in particular would take a shower, and then wrapped in a relatively small towel, sprawl on the living room couch and watch TV. We felt it was a conspiracy since others of them would pull similar antics walking around in their underwear and sexy nightees. They had to remain in sight of the inside surveillance team at all times, with exception of the bathroom. But, our staunch CID Agents managed to control themselves, and remained hidden.

At a party we threw for them after the operation, the gals all admitted that they had enjoyed themselves immensely, and in fact a few of them actually hooked up with some of the Agents.

For a while we were discussing terminating the operation, thinking that the perp, who was probably a member of the organization the husbands of the victims were a part, had been scared off. We stuck it out, and one night we hit paydirt. It was about 1130PM one night when one of the SF guys out in back of one of the houses observed a man, dressed in an Army fatigue work uniform sneaking around the rear of the quarters and appeared to be peeking into one of the bedrooms. He alerted the rest of the team, who were prepared to pounce. The plan blessed by our JAG, called for the perp to actually make an entry into the house before we did any pouncing. The man approached the kitchen door and knocked on it. This put everyone on overdrive, anticipating his next move. The gal we had in this house approached the door, and unlocked it and the would be rapist forciby entered into the laundry room which also concealed one of the Agents who pounced on the guy who knocked him down and ran from the quarters and headed into the nearby woods. (WRONG TURN). Being chased by the other agents who were in the house, and running towards the others who had been laying in the woods, the guy didn't have a chance in hell of getting away. In true SF fashion, the outside team sprang their ambush and low and behold, the misguided fool put up a fight. In all of the darkness, it cannot be explained, but the fool must have resisted arrest very strongly, and mindful of him carrying the Kabar knife, when dragged back out under the street lights, the perp looked like he had been run over by a large lawn mower. When interrogated several days later in the post hospital, he mumbled a confession, and also advised that he had scouted out two other houses we were working, but due to street traffic didn't approach them. The perp was in fact a member of the headquarters element of the unit whose wives were victimized, and he was aware of training schedules of all of the husbands, and thereby able to select his targets. All of the gals who were the backbone of the operation received letters of commendation from the Commanding Generals of both Ft Bragg, and the CID Command, as well as Army Commendation Medals for their part in his capture. The perp found himself on the wrong side of a General Courts Martial and was sentenced to spend the rest of his life in Leavenworth Prison.

As it was, he was arrested at a house which was about ½ mile from another set of quarters that I would, within the next year, become very familiar. This house was the scene of one of the most horrific murders imaginable and was the start of an investigation that followed me for the rest of my career. The exploits of our former SF Operators continued and they enjoyed the assignments, and were always ready to volunteer for the next one…That is until we started to have a chain of armed robberies in the parking lot of one of the NCO Clubs on the installation. The robbers had their plans as well, and they would sit in or around the parking lot waiting for someone who looked to be drunk, walking to his car. He would then be pounced upon and robbed. Some of the injuries were severe. We set up our counter-surveillance operation by hiding in the dense wooded area by the parking lot, and hopefully be able to grab the robbers as they pounced. One payday night as we watched the Club, one likely target of the robbers came stumbling into the parking lot, apparently attempting to get to his car. He approached a vehicle, and unlocked his door. He then thought better of it and then headed to the treeline where he proceed to unload his bladder before driving away. Well, laying in this particular parking lot in this particular treeline was one of our team. I was laying about 6 feet away from him watching what was about to unfold. Yes, you guessed it he began to pee into the treeline, directly onto my good friend the former SF troop named Paul C. (RIP) Being a disciplined SF trooper he didn't move or in any way give his position away. For this selfless act he was soaked by many beers which had been consumed by this unsuspecting soldier. After this our spectacular operations had a little less enthusiastic participation by other Agents. Well, not really. We also had a rash of strong arm robberies that occurred in a remote area of the post when the Saturday night drunk bus from Fayetteville would stop at a location on Highway 87, near a soldier living area which was about 100 meters from the bus stop if you walked through a heavily wooded area instead of staying on the walkway. Again, on a payday weekend, we set up in the woods to initiate what we called a "Rabbit" operation. This entailed waiting in the trees, sometimes literally in the trees, until someone would attempt to rob one of the MPs or CID Agents we had planted on the bus, who would walk or stagger through the woods in hopes of being accosted and robbed of a one dollar bill that we had planted in the wallet which we then gave to the victim. Once committed to the robbery we would spring out from our hiding place and inevitably begin a footchase to arrest the robber (Rabbit). Some nights when we operated this way we would arrest up to 5 or 6 robbers, who when searched would have the wallet with the one dollar bill in it. During one operation we set one of the CID Agents to be the hapless victim. As he stumbled through the woods he was approached from the opposite direction by a man on crutches. Oh well, it was only about 30 minutes till we called it a night. As the two walkers approached each other, the poor crippled man pulled a switchblade knife on our man and tried to rob him. Our man, who was told not to resist, and just give up the money, wanted to play hero and resisted, causing the robber to begin to beat him with one of his crutches. By the time the arrest team arrived at the scene, the robber had beaten him unconscious. This was more than a little bit embarrassing for the poor guy who had to try and live that one down. Being beaten and robbed by a man with a broken foot, and on crutches was not the manly way of doing things, even though the robber confessed and pled guilty at his courts martial.

BONNIE & CLYDE

In the 1970s, Ft Bragg was like any large city in America. It was full of people of different races, religions, and points of view, and, it was full of crime from both within and outside of the military reservation. The banks on Ft Bragg were scattered all over the inhabited parts of the post. With almost a published schedule, they were being subjected to armed robberies. Most of which were right on or around the military paydays. Both the CID and the FBI from the Fayetteville office began to stake out the banks with some success. There was one robbery which touched the hearts and souls of the MPs and CID. The payday stakeouts were in place across the post. A team of a male and a female robber entered the bank on the east side of the post leaving another couple of a male and female in a getaway car and pulled firearms and robbed the bank The silent alarm was triggered and lacking a good installation closure plan, all patrols, instead of forming a perimeter which would enclose the robbers, CID included, immediately raced to the bank. My partner that day was one of the former SF troops who was one of the agents who unsuccessfully clammered for shotguns or M-16s for the bank stake-out operation. We were told that probably nothing would happen and we didn't need all that armament.

As Jim K. and I slid around the corner near the bank we saw the getaway car screaming out of the parking lot and heading directly for us. We could see 4 people in the car and relayed the info that we had, and our direction of travel. The robbers had obviously scouted that area, and they headed for the nearest access road to NC 87, the major highway that ran north and south through the post. They were headed towards the Spring Lake area when they suddenly turned onto a dirt road that led to the Old post Cemetery. The dirt road led through a densely wooded area, and at a predetermined location, where they had placed a second getaway car they stopped and exited the vehicle. I know Clint Eastwood would never have done this, but this was to be our first major gunfight with bank robbers, so we can be excused. The bank robbers, as they ran for the fresh getaway car, unloaded on us with Mac 10 automatic weapons. Jim and I jumped into a ditch and without aiming we emptied our 2 inch barrel six shooters in the general direction of the bad guys & and girls, (2 each). This apparently gave them something to think about and they left us and got to their car and began their short lived escape.

Short lived but not short enough. They evaded the police and proceeded north to a small strip mall where they spotted a man alone near his car. They stopped by him and got out and carjacked him and the vehicle he was driving. The vehicle was a government owned vehicle, and the driver was a military police Investigator who was armed with, you guessed it, a .38 caliber snub nosed Colt. They drove with him and the getaway car to a dirt road just inside of the post and stopped at a wide spot on the road and began to viciously toy with him. They found his portable tape recorder and recorded some of the most horrible conversation I ever heard. They told him that he was a dead man, and his last minutes were coming up. All the while they were laughing and enjoying themselves. He begged for his life and they told him to record his last words to his wife and children. Those panic filled seconds will remain in my mind forever. They are too horrible to be repeated in this writing. . During an interrogation session I had with one of the female robbers I asked her what happened after that. She said that one of the male robbers, who she identified, took his gun and "Kilt the mother F*****" The NC State Police had set up a roadblock at a point several miles north of Spring Lake and when the killers tried to pass through it they were arrested. There was nothing lost when after their trial in which they gave each other up for a plea deal with the federal court the two males were sentenced to death. The way they killed the investigator was barbaric, and not as socially correct as their deaths were in prison. .

NEGLIGENT HOMICIDE (OR AGGRAVATED STUPIDITY)

꩜ ꧁

Negligent homicide occurs when someone, through gross negligence, causes the death of another. There were a number of occasions where I investigated such allegations. Two of these cases stand out due to their circumstances, and deadly consequences. Case# 1 took place in the remains of the old, world war 11 wooden barracks, a lot of which were still being used as living space for active military units in the 1970s. One such building was living space for the 612th Quartermaster Company which was being prepared to be vacated by the Quartermaster Company, to be used by the US Army Reserve when they came to Ft Bragg for their 2 weeks of summer camp. The preparation plan for this building included it being completely cleaned before the turnover. On this particular day it was the target of a good old fashion "GI Party" where a group of soldiers were to clean the building, under the supervision of a non-commissioned officer. In this case a Sergeant First Class. The work party of 12 men were broken into three groups. One each for the first and second floors of the sleeping area, and the third in the latrine. The floors in the latrine were quite dirty, and covered with patches of old paint that at one time was bright and shiny, and even waxed to make some other NCO happy before an inspection. The NCO in charge of this detail wanted to expedite the cleaning of this part of the building, and instructed the working crew to put down gasoline on the floor which he felt would loosen up the remaining paint and make it easier to clean it off. The remaining teams were trying to "spitshine" the rest of the barracks and were busy scrubbing floors and washing windows prior to the final inspection, which would then free them from this detail, and let them head into town for the weekend. The latrine detail was working hard to make their part of the cleanup suitable to their supervisor. They poured gasoline on the floors and were on hands and knees trying to scrape up the old paint when the NCO had the great idea to put some steel wool on an electric floor buffer, and make short work of that stubborn paint. By this time however, the fumes from all of the gasoline they used had permeated the entire building, and when the soldier who was to work the buffer, pressed the starting lever, a spark from the electric motor ignited the cloud of gas fumes and the entire building erupted in flames. Some of the workers managed to escape, and some were even rescued by others who were trying to escape. There were severe burns to almost all of the work detail, and even broken bones from jumping from the second floor fire escape. The truly unlucky men were those in the latrine. They received 2d and 3d degree burns, and a number of them sustained burn injuries that were fatal. One of those who escaped injury was the NCO supervisor.

I received the call from the MP Desk Sergeant while I was again the Duty Agent for the office. By the time I arrived, about 15 minutes after the call, the fire department, which was housed a short distance away had the flames out and were in the process of locating sets of human remains in what was left of the building. There were ambulances on scene and more were arriving to transport the injured, but still alive, to the hospital. One of the MP NCOs had the Sergeant First Class with him at his duty vehicle and was questioning him. It was obvious that the NCO was in a state of shock and medics were attempting to take him also to the hospital, but he was resisting, demanding that he be allowed to stay. I approached and learned from members of the Fire Dept that he was the NCO in Charge of the cleaning detail, and that he was standing in the doorway when the building exploded, knocking him to the street. I immediately stopped the MP NCO from talking with him anymore, and instructed him to take the NCO to the MP station and keep him under guard until I could get there and advise him of this rights. I called for backup from the CID office and within minutes had the entire office at the scene ready to assist. This was typical of CID Agents everywhere. They were always ready to assist with getting to the truth, by whatever means was necessary, no matter how gruesome the crime scene was. After about an hour on scene I had enough backround information to be able to brief the boss and to speak with the work detail NCO.

The NCO was still somewhat in shock, and I requested that an ambulance come and take him to the hospital for treatment by a doctor. I also learned that the hospital was arranging a medevac flight to pick up some of the most seriously injured, and transport them to a burn center. Four of their comrades had died from their injuries at the scene of the fire. That changed everything.

While waiting for the ambulance I read the NCO his rights, and had him sign a waiver so that I could talk to him before he was taken away. He was lucid, and agreed to talk to me to let me know exactly what had occurred. He told me what I took to be the truth since he was so matter of fact about what he had done, and his expression of pure guilt was all over him. It also matched what I had observed at the crime scene. He told me that it was all his fault and he had to make things right for the men on his work detail. He stuck with this mindset all of the way through his court proceedings where he pleaded guilty to the negligent homicide of those who didn't make it and for causing the injuries of those who did. I have never seen such a completely cooperative, and remorseful person who continuously disregarded the advice of his lawyers during his trial and while trying to make things right, cooperated completely with the General Courts Martial that held his future in its hands. I saw him openly cry when he learned that there were family members of those who died and were injured in the incident present in the courtroom. I spoke with him briefly before he was taken away by an MP escort to begin his prison sentence, and He introduced me to his mother and father who he had told previously that I was the case investigator who had treated him with respect, and that he trusted me completely. They were also tearful during this exchange and thanked me for treating their son so well. There are times like this very seldom encountered by CID Agents. I felt sorry for him and his act of aggravated stupidity on that Friday afternoon that led to so much misery, but I also felt sorrier for those who became victims.

The second memorable case was one of pure blood, guts, and dismemberment. I was again Duty Agent on another hot summer Friday afternoon, working again with another of our former SF troopers, James K. During the day we had responded to a number of minor larcenies, and an aggravated assault on an NCO by a soldier who was irked at the NCO for placing him on the KP roster for the following day which was a Saturday, thereby screwing up his whole weekend. The assault was with what is called a bunk adapter that makes one bunk into a double-decker. It seemed to be one of the favorite weapons of the 82d Airborne Division, and being made of steel, was highly dangerous. Jim and I were driving through the 82d area when we got a radio call to proceed to the Special Forces demolition range area for an unknown emergency. We made quick work of that drive, running code 3. When we rolled up on the scene, what we encountered was unbelievable. The demo range was arranged like an amphitheater with a few rows of stands and a control table, and downrange was about 50 yards below us on a sharp downgrade. I assumed the design was for safety. All over the range there were bodies, and parts of bodies scattered over the entire area. There were no signs of life in anyone in that down-range area. As I passed a GI combat boot standing alone, I looked at it and saw that there was part of a leg still in it. And this was just the beginning. As unbelievable as the scene was, we encountered a soldier near the roadway who was in shock, and we were told that he had been deafened by the explosion which threw him several feet from where he was standing behind another soldier. He was now waiting for an ambulance to take him to the Womack Army Hospital several miles away. That other soldier we learned, was kneeling over a ¼ lb block of C-4 when it exploded. At the uprange table we found the classes' company commander who offered the following information as to what occurred. I stayed with him, and Jim began to photograph the scene and all of its carnage. The Captain advised me that the dead soldiers were part of the Special Forces Training Group, who were in training to become Green Berets, and as a part of their training they were here to learn how to set what was described as a common series explosives circuit, A part of this session was for them to set a series of charges so that they simultaneously exploded when an electronic detonator was activated. The positions of the 13 dead soldiers, or at least the parts of them that lay all over the place indicated that they were at the point in establishing the circuit, where they placed an electric blasting cap into their explosives block thereby forming the circuit. The next step was for them to go to the top of the range area and observe the blast as it occurred when the final tie in of the wire was made to the detonator just prior to the switch being thrown detonating all of the charges set below. The wiring was supposed to have been checked by the instructor at the beginning of the class to insure that it was not "hot."

The only living member of this group, the man we saw up-range who had been deafened, was the instructor who, when questioned later, told me that as he stood behind the last student to complete the circuit, he saw him take the two ends of the wire that connected him into the circuit already established by the other students, and as he brought them together to tie them in, he saw the wire electronically arc which showed that the wire was indeed "HOT" causing the explosion to literally rip the class to pieces. From what remained of the others, it could be seen that there had not been a safety check of the up-range detonation point, which was immediately checked, and photographed, and the instructor acknowledged that he had assumed that the last class there had made the areas safe before leaving. 13 deaths later he was proven wrong. This was the most extreme of all blunders, which caused this NCO to be tried, convicted and sentenced to multiple years in prison. For an NCO, who had been proven in combat, to behave like this was inexcusable.

That explanation explained what was supposed to have occurred, but as we could all see, something went awry. To sum it all up, it was late on a Friday afternoon, and everyone was anxious to get through with this hands-on exercise, detonate their explosives, and return to the unit area and stand down for the weekend. Does this sound familiar? It was the same Friday afternoon rush that caused the fire in the quartermaster Company area. Safety has no timetable, and it was proven again.

The position or the remains of the class showed that some of the students had been bent over their charges, others had been holding the charges in their hands. This challenged the Pathologists at the hospital when trying to identify and associate different body parts with what was left of the torsos. With no DNA testing available, this proved to be a monumental task. While this case has been forever etched in my mind, it was not the worst. That was still to come.

BODIES EVERYWHERE

There seemed to be a dark cloud that hung over me at Ft Bragg. Almost everytime I was Duty Agent I came up with at least one body. At one point during the morning briefing to the boss, he mentioned that he was considering taking me off of the duty roster so that the death rate in the area could stabilize. He was kidding of course, don't you think??

Some of the other dead body calls ran like this:

On a Tuesday morning, just after the 4th of July long weekend, I got a duty call to come to the Bachelor Officer's Quarters where all of the single officers lived in a hotel like atmosphere. There had been a body found in one of the rooms. When my team arrived, we were greeted by a hysterical cleaning woman who, along with her boss, took us to a room where she told us that she approached about 20 minutes earlier, and noticed a strange smell coming from inside. She knocked at the door, and receiving no answer she opened the door with her pass-key in order to enter and clean the room. She said the smell was intense in the room and she went from the entry area into the bedroom she saw a nude man hanging from a closet door, apparently dead. She then freaked out and ran to the next building where she encountered her boss and then called the MPs.

When we arrived, we saw that the nude man had in fact hung himself from a closet which was facing the bed that had been covered with drawings, which were very good likenesses of several movie and TV stars of the time. All were nude, and were depicted as being bald, with nooses around their necks. This, coupled with the use of the towel suggested that this was an autoerotic, self-inflicted, accidental death. The corpse was that of a brand new second lieutenant, who was temporarily staying in this room and had checked in the day before the long weekend began. He had arranged himself on a chair directly in front of the closet, tucked the end of the towel over the top of the door, and then closed the door. He then took the other end of the towel and loosely tied it around his neck. He would then lean onto the towel, looking at the pictures he had displayed, choking himself to the point of passing out. This is when he would achieve his sexual fantasy, and ejaculate. What had happened is what I had seen in few other similar cases, where when leaning into the item wrapped around their necks, something had gone wrong and ooops, they passed out and hung themselves to death. We photographed the room with the body still hanging there, and then photographed and collected the pictures from the bed.

Once we finished we had the medics come in and remove the body. They were surprised to see it still hanging from the door in the position of death, and not laid out on the bed. They were trying to decide how best to remove it when one went behind the corpse, and held it by the waist, and another went to the front of it and held it under the armpits. While still trying to decide how to get him down, the third medic opened the closet door, releasing the towel and causing the body to drop straight down onto the floor. As the feet hit the floor the body didn't collapse due to rigor mortis having set in. the chain reaction then was for all of the pent up gases inside of the body to be expelled forcefully directly into the face of medic number two. He screamed and headed through the door to the hallway spewing what he had for breakfast all over everyone in his path. . The stench was horrid and we all made our way rapidly out of the building. On my way out I saw that at least one of the cleaning team had passed out. This was not the end of this case because the family of the deceased strongly disagreed with us on the cause of death and attempted to intimidate us into changing our report. General Officers, and congressman got involved, but we stood our ground.

If you think that one was a stinker, also on a hot July summer Monday morning, in a parking lot not far from the quartermaster Company fire scene, another unit was pulling police call in and around the parking lot, collecting all of the trash left there over the long hot weekend. One of the NCOs supervising the detail observed someone sitting in a Cadillac convertible, apparently sleeping. He approached the car and as he neared it he banged on the hood to wake the sleeper up. The sleeping man didn't move, and when the NCO got closer he noticed a smell that he had encountered in Vietnam; An over ripe corpse. The MPs were called and when they arrived they secured the scene and called for us. Accompanied by my partner, Bob Shaw, We went to the scene and began the formalities of declaring it a crime scene. Looking at the man in the car it was plain to see that he had a wound to the back of his head and that he was very dead. My partner opened the door and was the recipient of the results of two days of 100-plus degree heat in a closed space. I give him credit, he didn't act like the medic, or the cleaning lady in the BOQ.

Bodies attract cops, and so did this one. Members of the Drug Suppression team arrived to give the body a good look and recognized the car as belonging to a civilian heroin dealer from Fayetteville. They couldn't identify the body due to the condition it was in. But he was a civilian drug dealer. Lets call the FBI and DEA in on this one. While waiting for the Feds to arrive we continued our preliminary crime scene investigation and determined that the wounds in the back of the head looked like bullet holes, and that the brains had been liquefied by the intense heat, and were running out of the holes in the back of the head. By this time we were glad that the FBI would assume jurisdiction on this one and we wouldn't have to get inside of the stinking vehicle. We opened the other door of the car to help with the inside smell, which was getting worse by the minute. The FBI Agent who responded to the scene was an old friend of both of us and we had worked together on a number of cases, including other murder cases. While we briefed him on our findings to this point the medics arrived to take the body. There may have been times when I would be willing to assist them in moving a body, NOT THIS TIME!!! We could see the large blisters forming around his throat which indicated that gas gangrene had also set in. The medics were of the same mindset and didn't want to move the body, knowing that the stink had just begun. We didn't have to pull our guns on them, but we thought about it. Tom, the FBI Agent wasn't too happy about moving it either. At the end of our discussion the medics decided that they would take the body out of the car in stages. First the feet and legs and second the upper torso, and lay it on a stretcher before calling for a field ambulance so as not to completely foul the inside of their good ambulance. When they got the lower legs out of the car the gas gangrene blisters began to burst, and even in that open parking lot all of the soldiers who had remained to see what was going on began to run away. Can't blame them..the stink was overwhelming. Then something occurred then that stopped everyone in their tracks. As the legs came out of the car the pantlegs pulled up revealing that he had a number of small bindles of what looked like heroin taped to his legs. This put a stop to the corpse removal exercise, and his pants were slit with a knife exposing all of the bindles. Once we stopped and removed one bindle for a field test, we let the medics continue with the removal of the body, and had another CID team that had arrived escort the ambulance to the hospital where the Pathologist removed the other bindles and gave them to the accompanying CID Agents. This made the FBI Agent happy because this would allow him to call in the DEA to assist and possibly even assume on the investigation. All this took about 3 hours, and since our clothing was already a total loss from the smell, and Tom was a friend, we decided to stay with him and help him process the car. After all of the ground work had been done, and the DEA arrived at the scene we found that the driver of the vehicle was a major dealer in the Fayetteville area, and a DEA target of a widespread task force called Operation Eagle. He had run crossways with some other dealers and had been singled out for a hit. After being arrested, the people responsible said that they did it on post since they knew they wouldn't be interrupted in that isolated parking lot when they shot him. He had a total of 30 bindles taped to his legs, and was to deliver them to whoever had hit him. He had been shot three times in the back of the head from the rear seat, with a .22 cal. pistol and the hitman had been called in from Charlotte, NC. He was identified, arrested, and convicted of the murder. Another case solved.

All of the cases encountered were not solved within the first hour like on TV. many went unsolved, or at least unresolved. There was the case of the army wife who was brought in to the Army hospital around midnight by some people who brought her in to the ER and just left without identifying themselves or her. She of course was deceased. I just happened to be at the hospital making a security check since we had had some disturbances in the ER in recent weeks. I heard the nurses talking with a group of young doctors about the situation with the dead female. About that time a man entered the ER who claimed to be the husband of the deceased. He had a couple of other females with him. I took him aside and spoke to him, and he explained that the females with him had arrived at his home and told him his wife was at the ER, but he didn't know anything else about what had happened to her. I began to question one of the females about the situation, and she told me that the deceased was at an off post civilian hairdresser's shop to get an illegal abortion, and something had gone wrong. I went into the room where they body was laying on a guerney, and told the nurse what I had been told. The young doctors (probably just out of Med school) all chimed in saying that the dead woman was not pregnant based on them seeing her after she had been brought in to the ER nude. Seeing that continuing this discussion with them was going nowhere, I approached the

ER nurse and asked her to check for vaginal bleeding on the corpse. She did and found that her vagina had been packed with tissue and at that point I asked her to refrain from taking any out until the Pathologist could see her the next morning. She agreed. And as I walked out of the room, there wasn't a single word from any of the doctors. I located the beauty shop with the help of the females I spoke to earlier, and learned that one of the male operators in the shop routinely stayed late and performed coathanger abortions on females using the barber chairs. Since this was off post I decided to call the Sheriff's office and report it to them. They weren't interested in picking up the investigation. So I called the FBI duty guy and he also had no interest in it. I returned to the ER, told the husband what I had learned, and had to leave it at that. That was one of the cases that was solved but un-resolved.

Sometimes there is a case which is unfortunate but has a bit of comic relief to it. A single GI decided to end it all and he climbed a huge cottonwood tree, placed a noose around his neck and jumped. This caused a number of things to occur. The neck of course broke, and the blood was profuse. None of the responding medics wanted to climb the tree and cut the body down. A female Staff Sergeant assigned to the post photo office, who was thought of as being quite odd, said that she would be glad to volunteer to climb the tree and cut the body down. As I watched her I could see that she was a few cans short of a six-pack. She was dressed in her uniform which was a skirt and a blouse, and as she began to climb the tree it was clear that that was all she had on. One of the medics on scene was a female and she called up to the half nude climber that she should come down. The photo gal replied to her that if you don't like it don't look. Oh yes, to complete the scene, it was around midnight and we had some large light sets from the engineers illuminating the tree, and what a sight it was.

There was a case that was unfortunate and pitiful. I responded to a report of death at a family quarters on the post. Upon arrival I learned that the woman of the house, who over the past months had been deeply depressed, had locked herself in the family bathroom, and had shot herself in the head. Death had not been immediate and the husband had to break down the bathroom door, and try to give her first aid. The heartbreaking part of it all was when I arrived, the husband and a child about 10 years old were sitting on the curb in front of the house, and the father was trying to explain to the boy why this had happened.

Another death that surfaced which also involved a small child occurred in the barracks where all of the Female soldiers, or WACs lived. In one room which was shared by two WACs there was a strange and foul odor coming from one of the girls's wall lockers. The owner of the wall locker was away on a 3 day pass, and would not return for 2 more days. When the Company Commander of the WACs had the lock cut and opened the locker she found a small bundle of blankets that held the dead body of a newborn child. The bundle was carried out of the room and brought to the porch on the first floor. The MPs were called first and when they saw what was in the blankets they immediately called me. When I opened the bundle I saw that the tiny newborn child had been in the wall locker for some time, and the mid-section was infested with maggots. Since the child was obviously a civilian, I called the FBI and made the appropriate notification of a civilian death on the military base. The FBI Agent who responded was one with whom I had worked several times. As we began to dig into the backround of the case we learned that although several of the other WACs assigned here, including the roommate, knew that the owner of the wall locker had been pregnant up until about a week ago, no one had notified the Company Commander since it would have been an automatic General Discharge from the Army, which the girl did not want. How they figured it could be kept secret was anybody's guess. I called the Army hospital and spoke to one of the pathologists there and he responded also to the scene. When he saw the condition of the body, he said that it must have been stillborn, and had been in the wall locker for about two weeks. The FBI Agent arranged for the WAC who was on pass to be arrested at her home on a charge of wrongful disposal of a human body, and brought back to Ft Bragg. When she returned and was questioned she said that she panicked when the child was born, and didn't know what to do with it so she wrapped it up and locked it her locker, and then requested a 3 day pass so she could go home and tell her mother what had happened. After that incident there was a wholesale clearance of the WAC Company up to and including the Company Commander. The local US Attorney refused to take the case to the Grand Jury since the mother of the dead child had been discharged from the Army. Another weird ending for another weird case.

THE BIG ONE!!

There were other death investigations, but these were some of the more memorable. The most memorable of all of the death investigations, Drug deals, robberies or any other unlawful act that I or most other CID Agents have encountered occurred on a rainy Tuesday night, the 17th of February 1970, in one of the company grade officers housing areas on Ft Bragg. Ft Bragg was like any large city. It was a thriving metropolis, full of life and purpose during the daytime, and at night it held the potential for witnessing man's inhumanity to men, or in this case, to one's own family. One of the city's streets in Fayetteville was very aptly nicknamed "Combat Alley."

On this very fateful night, I was again blessed, or cursed to be the CID Duty investigator for the installation. It was a 24 hour stint of answering calls from all sorts of people seeking information, reporting crimes, and passing data required by other agents. The Duty room was the heart and soul of the whole CID Operation. This particular day was no different than any other duty day. I answered calls of assaults, larcenies, lost weapons, and many more. It was a busy day, which made it pass all that much quicker until 0730 in the morning, when I would be relieved by the Operations Officer, and the on-coming Duty

Investigator. That is of course life under normal conditions. This duty day would prove to be anything but normal.

The Provost Marshal, or Military Chief of Police, who, for an installation the size of Ft Bragg, was a full Colonel also had an investigative operation of what was called Military Police Investigators (MPI). These soldiers who also had a duty investigator, handled all misdemeanor complaints, while the CID concentrated on felony cases, or those whose punishment was for at least one year in confinement.

The Duty Agents room was in the main administrative area of the office, and consisted of the duty Agent's desk and telephone, The MP/CID radio dispatch equipment, a teletype machine with which we kept our higher headquarters in Atlanta, Ga apprised of our daily investigative activities, and a small room with a bunk that, given the opportunity, we could catch a nap between calls in the evening (Yeah, right).Our investigative equipment was a Speed Graphic press camera, a smaller Polaroid camera, a fingerprint kit, and whatever equipment we could scrounge which would assist us in processing a crime scene, such as different sized pill vials and plastic bags to hold evidence, forceps and other medical/dental tools that we obtained from the hospital that were invaluable when picking up evidence, and of course Sherlock Holmes favorite tool, the detective's magnifying glass. All this was packed in a large briefcase with pens, pencils, paper for sketching, markers for marking evidence containers, and all was kept handy for action if needed, and oh boy, would they ever be needed during this night.

The MPI Duty guy for that night, was Tony R. who I had pulled duty with a few times before and he was known to me to be a dependable, and knowledgeable investigator. We worked in different buildings which were close to each other, but had teamed up before on cases, and this day was no different. The MPI Duty Investigator was under the operational control of the CID Office during the non-duty hours.

Our day had been busy with no major cases coming in, but a lot of cases which were comparatively minor in nature which had been referred to the office. I had received in the mail a number of requests for assistance from other CID offices around the world requesting assistance with cases they had opened such as Vietnam War Crimes allegations, fraud cases, and others. It was enough to keep me busy throughout the day, and well into the evening. Tony's day over at MPI had been pretty much the same. I didn't stop until well after midnight and when I looked at the duty bunk, I could feel it calling to me. I crawled onto the bed, hoping to catch just a few winks before the end of my shift when I had to brief the office on what had occurred the previous day. One thing that was mentioned to me by the boss before he left the previous evening was "No Bodies, right"?? My response to him was "Right Chief". Maybe I shouldn't have given that answer.

While resting on the bunk, I really didn't sleep, but kept that duty agents edge while unconsciously monitoring the MP radio net. Once grounded in police work, and having ridden in radio cars for years, one will have the unit's radio on for a full shift, but only really hear it when either the unit's radio call sign is used by the dispatcher, or if a patrol or another unit encounters an emergency situation and the excitement is passed through his, or her voice pattern.

It was sometime after 0340 when this happened on the MP net. The conversation was pitched so that it was obvious that something major had occurred. I listened and heard calls from patrols that had been dispatched into the housing area, that told me that a stabbing attack on someone had occurred. I got onto the net and asked the patrol if there were any fatal injuries at the scene. The MP answered, yes. I advised that I would be enroute. I immediately called my MPI backup, T. R, and told him to meet me at my office and that we were responding to a stabbing call. My second call was to the office photographer.

The photographer was a Staff Sergeant, who was not an MP or CID Agent, who had been assigned to us as a favor to his previous commander who had no use for a photographer and wanted to help us out. He was a great guy who was good with the Speed Graphic camera and could photograph any inanimate thing we needed photographed such as the entry place on a burglary, tire tracks on the ground, etc. He had no experience however, in photographing scenes of violence.

Tony R. and I got into my duty car, and proceeded to the scene where the MPs had called from. It took barely 5 minutes and we arrived at 0400. While it had been raining heavily earlier in the day, when we arrived it was a softer rain when we walked from the car to the house which bore the address of 544 Castle Drive. There were MPs at the front door, and we walked past them and into the living room of the house. I saw the MP Duty Officer, the representative of the Provost Marshal, standing not far from the door, and I approached him and asked him what had occurred. He stated that he and the other patrols had responded to the calls from the initial patrol on scene that had requested assistance. When they arrived they had found the front door closed, and had gone to the back door which they found unlocked and open. When they entered they found a man, who they thought was the resident, and a woman who was apparently dead, sprawled on the master bedroom floor. As he spoke I saw that the living room had been the location where some violence had apparently taken place. The coffee table next to the couch had been knocked over and was resting on its side. There were some magazines and a potted plant laying next to the table. At the opposite side of the living room there was a hallway which ran to the back of the house, and I saw some medics rolling a guerney down the hallway and through the living room to the front door. The Duty Officer stated that that the man laying on the guerney was the man who they thought was the resident. He was a white man who appeared to be unconscious, or at least had his eyes shut. I then saw that there were two MPs at the far end of the hallway. I asked the MPDO how many MPs were at this scene and where were they. He then grabbed an NCO and began placing the MPs so they could secure the house and the entrances. He at that time also set up a check point where they could restrict entry to persons arriving at the front door of the house. . I asked him to continue with his briefing and he took me to the hallway and we walked to the far end which ended at the doorway to the master bedroom. We stood at the doorway and he told me that the body that was laying just a few feet from the doorway was apparently the wife of the resident who had been taken out of the house and placed in an ambulance for transport to the hospital. While I was taking this all in, the Lt told me that there was more, and he took me back into the hallway and to two nearby bedrooms. He pointed into one of the rooms with a flashlight, and I saw the light switch on the wall and assuming my crime scene protection mode, I took a ballpoint pen and flipped the switch on. I could see a small child all covered up in bedding laying there. She was bloody and I thought, apparently dead. He also took me across the hallway to another bedroom and I flipped the lights on there as well. I saw laying in a bed, another small child who I also assumed to be dead. There was blood all over the body, the bed, and the floor alongside of it. The Lt said that was all they found. We returned to the living room and I saw that Tony R. was talking to some of the medics and MPs who had been there when we arrived. It was a bit difficult to take the scene all in and I knew that I was going to have to have a lot of help to get through this. I went to the next door apartment and met the resident who was standing on the landing in front of his apartment. He identified himself and I asked him if I could use his telephone to make a number of calls and he quickly took me into his house where I called the Chief of the Ft Bragg CID Office, and explained what I had found to that point. He said he was on the way, and that I should call anyone I wanted to help and have them report immediately to the crime scene. I then called everyone I could think of to come and assist. I then asked the resident if he would accompany me back to the crime scene and see if he could positively identify the bodies I had found there. He said yes and we returned to the other apartment and as we walked through, stopping at the doorway of each bedroom, he identified them as Collete, the mother, Kimmy and krissy, the two daughters of Cpt Jeffrey MacDonald, the man who had been rolled out of the house on the gurney. Shortly after this, When I was in the master bedroom trying to absorb all that was in front of me, my backup Agents began to arrive. The first was an old friend and a former SF trooper Paul C. He was followed by Bob S. I assigned Paul to process the bedroom on the north side of the house where the smaller of the girls lay in her bed. I had worked enough with him to know that he wouldn't miss anything. Bob and I started on the master bedroom, thinking that it was probably the most complex of all of the three bedrooms, and it was. The body was sprawled on the bedroom floor, and had obviously been beaten savagely on the head and arms with the arms being obviously broken as she attempted to defend herself. At the foot of the body there was a green and blue throw rug that had on it a blue pocket from a pajama shirt. About this time, other Agents who had been notified of the situation by the CID office started arriving and looking for something to do to assist with this monumental crime scene. Most of them I sent to the office for further reassignment and others to start on a neighborhood check to see if anyone else in the area had any information about what had occurred. The photographer had also arrived and I assigned him to start in the living room and photograph everything in a clockwise fashion, and to include everything he saw. He said OK and began to photograph the scene now that most of those who were there had departed. It wasn't long until I saw him walking around the house looking like he was one of the victims. He was obviously affected by what he had seen. I approached him and asked how he felt. He muttered that he was about to be sick. I immediately got him out of the house and told him to return to the CID office. Knowing that I needed a quality photographs of this scene, I called Mr Jim who was the chief of the Installation photo lab. Jim and I had worked a number of other violent death scenes, such as the one at the WAC Barracks, written above, and he was very capable of handling this one. He lived very close by and within 15 minutes he was there with his professional equipment. I walked him through the scene and then set him to photograph the entire house. He knew what was needed and he began. That was one of my better choices that morning. The photos he produced were beyond my hopes.

Returning to the master bedroom I found that Bob, realizing that it would take a team to process the room, had jumped to the bedroom on the north side of the house where the larger of the girls was also laying in her bed. He told me what he had found to that point and that he was already Marking some pieces to be picked up and sent to the CID Crime Lab in Georgia, such as drawing the outline of the girl's body with his marker on the bottom sheet on the bed. The child was seen to be laying on her left side and was tucked in all around her with blankets from the bed, looking as if she had been killed in her sleep. That would quickly be reassessed in just a short period. She had been struck across the head with a weapon such as the bloody 31 inch length of 2x2 that had been found laying on the ground just outside of the rear door to the laundry room and master bedroom, and then stabbed repeatedly with a knife on the right side of the neck so many times it wasn't possible to count the knife wounds there. There appeared to be a lot of hate and frustration involved in that stabbing. Also laying on the bottom sheet there were wood splinters probably from the club, which was positively tied to the house by the crime lab. Also found on or near the body were a number of dark blue threads that did not match any clothing on the body, or from any of the bedding. These items were also picked up and placed in some of the pill vials that I had brought in the crime scene kit. Masking tape was then placed on the vial and it was marked for evidence. At this point we knew that there would be multiple items of potential evidence that would be taken from the house and we devised an identification system to insure they were not mixed and could be singled out if necessary. The rooms were then named NBR: North Bed room, SBR: South bedroom, MBR: master bedroom, etc and items picked up would then be further identified as items 1, & 2 NBR, 1& 2 SBR etc. It became a godsend that we set this procedure since there were literally hundreds and hundreds of items that we sent to the lab and eventually entered into evidence at the grand Jury and at trial. The SBR room turned out to be the quickest of all the rooms in the house to process, and it was one which early on, put us on the right track. Key pieces of evidence found were the blue threads on the bottom sheet, blue threads under the pillow, and bloody slivers of wood that would compare positively to the wooden club. Also, during the autopsy conducted at the installation hospital, it was noted that the left cheek of the body had been struck also by the club, fracturing the cheek, and breaking the nose. But that was the side of the body that was on the downward side, next to the bottom sheet. How then could this have happened if she were killed in her bed and then made to look as if she had been killed while neatly tucked in. The words "set up" quickly ran through our heads. We took a quick break and I went to the next door apartment and called the "Chief" at the office and briefed him on what we had initially found, and asked him if he could get a team from the Crime Lab to respond to the scene, and assist in what was quickly becoming a major production. He called me back in about 30 minutes and stated that he had arranged for a team from the CID Crime Lab in Georgia be on the ground by mid-day, and that the 4 Star Commanding General had already dispatched his private plane to pick them up. This was becoming a first team assault on the crime scene.

We returned to our processing of the scene, and Bob and I continued with the master bedroom. On the shag carpeting that the woman's body was laying on, I observed a profusion of dark blue threads all along the side off the body, and that laying on top of the chest area of the body there was a torn light blue pajama top that was bloody, and across the abdomen was a white towel like item later identified as a Hilton hotel bath mat that was lightly bloodied with stains that looked like sharp objects such as cutting instruments (Knives) had been wiped off. The pajama shirt was laying partially hiding several knife wounds. The brutality of the attack on this woman was unimaginable. The left arm of the body was extended above the head and next to the hand I spotted a small piece of what looked like clear rubber. All these items I mention were picked up, and marked and packaged as evidence. I continued to process the immediate area around the body, and the next item I went to was a bundle of bedding that had been bundled up and thrown on the floor not far from the hallway door. The bedding had apparently been ripped from the double bed in the room and the bottom sheet which was still on the bed had a wet spot on it. I began to open the bundle of bedding when I noticed that there was a lot of blood on the sheets, which make me glad that I had surgeons gloves on. As I dug deeper into the bundle I found more pieces of clear rubber similar to the gloves I had on. Each one was picked up and placed in a different pill vial. One piece was an entire finger section of a bloody latex glove. The rest of the bundle was then put into a plastic trash bag, to be reopened under lab conditions by a lab technician. I continued to process around the body and the bed and about that time a medical team that had been called to take the bodies to the morgue arrived. Paul, Bob, and I conferred and decided that we had processed the bodies to our satisfaction and that the bodies should be taken to the awaiting pathologists for autopsy. I accompanied the medical team as they took each body from where we had found them and placed them on stretchers. When they came to the body of the woman I took particular attention to what they were doing since earlier I had spotted some object sticking out of a large blot clot under her head. As they lifted the body I saw that it was another of the dark blue threads seen earlier around the body, this and others which had been hidden under the body were collected. This collection of the threads was bothering me. As I continued, I went to the bedside where the murderer had written in blood the word PIG. It was written from the top of the headboard to the mattress top. As I was there, I looked behind the headboard and saw on the floor, more of the blue threads laying there. We also found that laying on the floor partially hidden by the dresser, was a paring knife that appeared to be bloodied. As we found items like this, which we felt would explain to us what had occurred, we called Jim the photographer in to photograph each item as we found it. This included other murder weapons which were just outside of the rear door such as the club, another paring knife, and an ice pick, the wounds from which were very evident on the chest areas of the smaller girl, and the mother. The mothers ice pick wounds were from a vicious hateful attack, and the 3 year old girl's were just like pin pricks, barely breaking the skin.

The savagery showed however with the knife wounds to the baby. She was stabbed multiple times on the chest, and then held over the side of the bed, and probably over her father's lap, and stabbed again multiple times in the back. There was also one stab wound that apparently was a defense wound to her hands. One of her fingers was punctured by a knife indicating that she was trying to put her hand between the knife and her chest. The concensus was that she had been killed only because she was old enough to tell us that daddy had hurt mommy, It was for his own protection that she was sacrificed. Later, when being interrogated, the only emotion that he showed was when he was answering a question about the younger girl Kristen (Krissy). As can be seen, the crime scene was extremely complex, but let's return to the Master Bedroom and the evidence being collected there. Directly inside of the bedroom, and in front of the door, there was a large blood stain which had penetrated through the shag carpet, showing that whoever had lost that blood had to be laying there for however long it took for that quantity of fluid to sink to the bottom of the shag. Certainly several minutes.

In the meanwhile, the lab team had arrived from Georgia, and were waiting for instructions on their role in the crime scene. They represented the entire lab with representatives from the fingerprint, chemistry, and photo sections. They were all cross trained to some extent and could function without an Agent accompanying them. After taking them on a guided tour of the house I let them do what they do best. I broke them down so as to have their expertise throughout the scene. The Chemistry rep went to the kitchen, the photo rep again began to photograph both inside and outside of the house. The fingerprint rep started in the kitchen and when last seen was slinging fingerprint powder over everything he felt could hold a fingerprint. I returned to the master bedroom and rejoined

Bob. Paul, who had finished in the North bedroom of Krissy came with me and we continued with the collection of the evidence that had been identified as crucial, such as the murder weapons, additional blue threads, and the bedding from the floor and bed. While doing this, Paul advised that he had found similar blue threads on Krissy's bed as well.

The Chemistry rep who had been working in the kitchen reported that he had collected bloodstains from the floor and sink, and that he had studied a circular pattern of blood spots which were directly in front of the sink and the cabinet doors to the space under the sink. The spots, according to his educated calculations had fallen directly downward from a height of about 18 inches. Apparently from a source of blood in some quantity. It probably came from someone who was bending over and reaching into the space beneath the sink. I then went to that cabinet, opened it, and found along with cleaning supplies, a box of Perry latex surgeon's gloves. The box was also marked and collected as evidence. A pattern was beginning to form.

The documenting and collection of evidence continued with the Lab team for a week, followed by two more weeks of the original processors from the Ft Bragg CID, myself included. Nothing was too insignificant to be taken for additional analysis by the investigative crew, and everything imaginable was scrutinized and collected if it showed anything of interest to the crew. While the lab crew was still at the scene, I joined one of the fingerprint reps and went to the living room, and processed it. There was a couch along the east wall and next to it, laying on its side was heavy wooden coffee table. When we finished processing this area I went back to the table and attempted numerous times to get the table to rest on its side.

It was so top heavy that it kept rolling and ended up flat on its top. When found, the table had rested on a small pile of a children's game, and a copy of Esquire Magazine which featured the cover story of the Tate/Labianca murders in Hollywood which were committed by Charles Manson and his cult followers. The story told in great detail what was found at those crime scenes, including the printing in blood of the word "PIG" like what was written on the Macdonald headboard in the master bedroom. While inspecting the magazine a bloody smudge, in the configuration of a finger was found on the top edge of the pages it looked like someone had opened the book and selected story items and used them to set up the crime scene we were working. The story given by Macdonald to the CID Agents while he was at the Womack Army Hospital was that he had been sleeping on the couch when he heard his wife screaming "Jeff, Jeff, why are they doing this. That's not far from "Jeff, Jeff, why are you doing this", and at the same time he heard Kimmy crying Daddy, Daddy, Daddy. At that time he stated that he was being attacked by a group of about 4, including one female.The males had what he thought was a baseball bat and a knife, the female was holding a candle chanting "Acid is groovy, Kill the pigs. This is also similar to the Hollywood murders outlined in the Esquire Magazine. He stated that It was during this attack that his light blue pajama top was ripped up the front and ended wrapped around his wrists. It was this pajama top which he later put onto the chest area of his wife when he stated he found her body on the master bedroom floor. With the alleged initial assault having taken place between the couch and the coffee table, it stands to reason that there would be some signs of a fight in that space, but none was found. The fingerprint rep and

I crawled on our hands and knees all over that carpeted attack area looking for anything foreign to it, like threads from the pajama shirt, blood stains, or anything. What we came up with was what you would find on any carpet in a house with children, but nothing connected to an assault. There were no threads from a torn pajama shirt or anything that would suggest that a violent fight had taken place there. According to Macdonald, he had struggled with them hitting him with the club and also stabbing him in the side, until they arrived at the entrance to the hallway which ran from the living room to the master bedroom. It was at his point that he said that he fell unconscious at the end of the hallway. A search for any significant amount of blood was made there with negative results. There was only a trace of blood that was too small to be typed at the lab. But yet, we find Macdonald's blood in the kitchen and on the sink in front of the bathroom mirror, near the master bedroom in some quantity, but nothing compared to what was found on or near the 3 dead females. Something was seriously flawed with his story.

Each night when we finished working for the day we would consolidate what we had collected in a central place in the house, and then lock and seal the doors, and leave the house under the watchful eyes of an MP patrol which was permanently stationed outside of the house. This also was used to satisfy the requirement of a chain of custody of all evidence. It was determined that we had established what is known as "constructive custody". While it may seem that we were collecting items throughout the house with no rhythm or reason, that could not be farther from the truth. Each item, be it a suspected murder weapon, or an insignificant trace of a blood stain, It was collected based on the excellent training we had received, or the extensive experience of the Special Agents on scene. In most of the cases it was both. We shall see, as the case progresses, and once we started to receive results from the Crime Lab That the evidence we found, or saw that was absent from the scene, began to fill in many of the blanks that had us scratching our heads.

I don't know what the odds are but we were blessed with bonus card that gave us a family of 4 with 4 separate and distinct blood types: Colette: A, Jeffrey B, Kimberly AB, and Kristen O. This would enable us to show movements throughout the house of those injured people. It would also show us the activities of the family members up to, and until, their final resting places. This is something I'm sure that the husband, father, and killer of the victims didn't calculate on as he read the esquire magazine that night while trying to emulate the Manson bunch. This is exactly one of the major miscalculations that resulted in Jeffrey Macdonald, being found guilty of 2 counts of 2d degree and one count of 1st degree murder.

Let me revisit each room of the house where we collected key pieces of evidence, or where we didn't find evidence where it should have been if Macdonald's story were true. Later we shall explore what the crime Laboratories (CID, FBI, and US treasury Dept) tell us what their examination of the items of evidence showed.

In the Master bedroom we found one of the knives used in the killings, a bundle of bloody bedding which contained bloody sections of a latex surgeons glove, Additional pieces of a bloody surgeons glove found on the floor near the body of Colette, bloody seam threads from a pajama shirt identified as belonging to J. Macdonald were found all around, and under the body of Colette, under the bed covers from Kimberly's bed where she was found all neatly tucked in, behind the headboard of the master bed, and on the body of Kristen. On the green and blue throw rug upon which Collete's feet rested, the bloodstained pocket torn from the husbands pajama top was also found.in addition to purple cotton seam threads from his pajamas. The throw rug is not far from the section of the shag carpet that was heavily stained with Kimberly's type AB blood. If this is a lot to comprehend at this point, I'll try to clarify with some of the lab results.

The paring knife found by the dresser in the master bedroom was positively identified by a frequent babysitter as being one that she washed many times while doing her babysitting chores in the house. Another paring knife found just outside of the rear door, partially hidden under a large bush was similarly identified by the babysitter. The profusion of dark blue seam threads which were found near, or under all of the bodies, were positively identified as originating from the blue pajama shirt Macdonald admitted to placing on the chest area of his dead wife. The pocket found by her foot also was at one time a part of the same shirt. However, while the remnants of the shirt that lay on the body was saturated in the mother's blood, the pocket which had been ripped from it had barely been stained with blood. The bundle of bedding found on the floor after being torn from the master bed was extensively stained with the blood of the entire family. How could his have happened? The FBI Crime Lab in Washington DC examined the bedding and the pajama shirt and advised us that the pajama shirt had been stained twice with Collete's blood. Once before and the second time after it was ripped down the middle. The bedding which was stained with the blood of Collete, Kimmy, and Krissy also had imprinted on it in Collete's blood, an impression of the seam of the pajama shirt. Which tells us that while the crime scene was being set up, the husband and father carried the bloody body of Collete while transporting it from one room to another. This will become so much clearer after I put forth the theory that was established, and offered to the trial jury during trial. One thing that should be added here is that Krissy's bed sheet was heavily stained with blood, from direct bleeding from Collete. Something that was developed by the handwriting section of the Army Crime Lab was that the word "PIG", written on the headboard of the bed in the master bedroom was written in Colletes blood, by a right handed person, using the first two finger of the right hand. The writer had to return to the source of the blood several times in order to finish the writing. The hand was covered with a thin substance, since there were no traces of fingerprints on the writing. What could possibly have covered this hand? Perhaps the surgeons gloves found in the kitchen, and fragments of them found in the master bedroom in the bundle of bedding and on the floor by Collete's body. The US Treasury Dept in Washington, DC also has a crime lab. The fragments of latex gloves, and the intact gloves found under the kitchen sink, next to the blood of Jeffrey Macdonald were submitted to them for examination of their chemical content, which showed them to be identical.

With each report received from the Crime Labs working on our case, more of our questions which had been formed during our crime scene processing were being answered, and all of the answers pointed directly at Jeffrey Macdonald.

The south bedroom, or that of Kimmy, was processed by Bob S. and myself. This was the least disturbed room. The body of Kimmy, as stated earlier was laying on the left side, and was neatly tucked in around the body. The horrendous wounds to this tiny body were filled with emotions seen in earlier crime scenes, which were those of hate, and deliberation. The pathologists who performed the autopsies, surmised that the first blow to the child, had been to the left cheek, which rendered her unconscious. She fell to the floor and bled extensively onto the carpeting in the master bedroom doorway. Whether at this point she was dead or alive is conjecture.

This blow had fractured the cheek, broken the nose, and deviated it to the right. Now comes the question, how could this be if she was found laying on her left side, and all tucked in with this cheek not being exposed to the attacker. Here a picture would be worth a thousand words. The majority of the injuries to Kimmy were to the right side of her head and cheek and the right side of her neck and throat. Here is where the hate, frustration, and deliberation of the assailant show themselves. The cheek had been bludgeoned repeatedly with the wooden club found outside of the rear door, and the neck had been stabbed so many times that it was impossible to count the times the paring knife had been used on her. The ferocity of the attacks on Kimmy and on Collette cannot be accurately described here. It was unthinkable that a grown man could have inflicted the beatings and stabbing that these two lovely ladies in this fashion. We tied the wooden club to this attack by finding bloody splinters from it that were found under the undisturbed pillow on the right side of Kimmy's bed, and positively matched to the club. And let us not forget the pajama top seam threads which were found under Kimmy's bedding after they had been pulled down when we first viewed the body. The threads seem to pop up everywhere in the crime scene, except for that area in the living room where Macdonald claims he was attacked by the hippie-like intruders, who supposedly ripped his blue pajama top from his body and left it hanging from his wrists by the cuffs. Listing, and describing the locations where we found the seam threads would take an entire chapter of this writing. The FBI Crime Lab in Washington, DC did some amazing work with the evidence, especially the pajama shirt. They analyzed the ice pick puncture holes in the shirt and reported that all of the holes were perfectly symmetrical, and were from thrusts when the pajama shirt was immobile, and if Macdonald was wearing it he would look like a pin cushion. Also, they found that the shirt had been stained, in Collete's blood, twice with a heavily bleeding person, obviously Collete, in or on it. Once before and once after it had been torn down the middle. Now, where could this have happened?

The North Bedroom, or that of Krissy was much different. It was filled with blood soaked items such as the bed which of course was stained with Krissy's blood, also had a top sheet which was heavily stained in Colette's type A blood. The floor at her bedside was also covered with Krissy's blood where she had been pulled over the side of the bed and had bled heavily. On the ceiling and walls of the room there were blood trails where an object,(the wooden club??) covered in Colettes blood had sprayed the blood on the walls when the object was swung in a downwards direction. (Oh yes, analysis of bloodstains is a learned trait for investigators.) There were two distinct bloody footprints leading away from the bed and the body of Krissy, and another more smudged foot print leading into the hallway. As with Kimmy, the body had been repositioned as to give the impression that she had been killed in her sleep, and had stayed tucked in. A babies plastic drinking bottle containing what looked like chocolate milk, lay inches from her mouth. What looked like a defensive stab wound was seen on one of Krissy's fingers as her hand lay on her chest. this indicated that on the underside of that finger there was a corresponding knife wound to her chest from that same stab wound. There was an array of children's toys, a rocking horse and other objects you would expect to find in a small child's room. In fitting all those pieces of evidence just described with the growing theory tells us a story of a depraved, and panicking mind. It took months for all of the crime lab work to be done in Georgia, but about 6 weeks after the murders, we had a surprise visitor to the CID Office. Cpt Jeffrey Macdonald, in his fatigue uniform, walked in to the office wanting to get back into the house and to have his possessions released back to him from the house. We were awaiting some key lab results before we had a confrontational session with Macdonald, but the opportunity was there and we seized upon it.

The CID Chief, Joe G, Bob Shaw, and myself invited him in to the Chief's office, and Joe began the session by reading him his rights. His response to this was" Wow,That's sounds Ominous". He waived his right to an attorney, and when asked, began to relate the well worn story of the hippie intruders attacking him and his family. We let him ramble and then began to ask pointed questions for which he didn't have satisfactory answers. His answers however were cold and calculated, and the only time he got emotional whatsoever, was when he was talking about the

Baby; Krissy. When speaking about Collete or Kimmy he was cold and stone faced. We kept at it for about 4 hrs when he asked for a break. Before we terminated the session Joe asked him if he would submit to a polygraph examination. He answered in the affirmative. He was told to be back in the office at 1300. By the time he walked from the CID office, the short distance to the BOQ, where the Lt was found hanging the previous July, he called back and told us that he had changed his mind about the polygraph. That was too bad since we had arranged for the US Army's Polygraph Guru in Washington to come down and he was scrambling to get a flight to Ft Bragg to conduct the exam himself. Oh Well, it was back to pounding the pavement to get our answers. And pound we did. This hearing was damaging to our morale, but after thinking about it, and the status of our evidence which was pointing directly at Macdonald, we decided that this may be a blessing and that now we had time to refine our evidence into a more presentable state. The first thing we needed was an organizational structure to ensure our hard work was not in vain. We formed an investigative Task Force called TF 9191, and moved to the Federal Building in Fayetteville where we could spread our evidence and documents and be sure that it was secure. By this time an Investigating Officer was appointed by the Commanding General to see If there was sufficient evidence to convene a General Courts Martial. It is the equivalent of the civilian Grand Jury. After we parted from the interrogation of Macdonald, he, or his family acquired civilian Lawyers to represent him in the case. They descended on Ft Bragg like Sherman descended on Georgia. A hearing was rapidly convened and the evidence collected and processed by the Crime Lab was presented to the Investigative Officer who was an Infantry Colonel, with no legal training at all.

The defense lawyers seized upon the moment and turned the hearing into what can only be described as a three ring circus. It was relatively easy to predict the outcome of this mismatched contest, After hearing all of the evidence we had, and with not knowing what had not been presented, The untrained Colonel pronounced a verdict of not guilty for Macdonald. This was not what he was appointed to do, he was only to rule if there was sufficient evidence to hold him for a court proceeding. The Defense team however, ran with the ball that was passed to them, and made press releases that they felt would exonerate him. We in CID were livid about this, but were instructed to Not Comment if asked.

When we started to get the meat of the lab work results in, we started in earnest having brain sessions concerning what we had collected and all of its implications. While working at the crime scene one day we were visited by several FBI Agents accompanied by the Senior Resident Agent (The Big Boss) from Charlotte, NC who was given a tour of the house, with a very candid briefing on what we had found there. He was impressed, and stated that he had brought some of his best men with him in case we needed any help, but was amazed at how thorough we had been and said that it was the best crime scene processing that he had ever seen, noting that he would not have expected his men to do such a meticulous job. That made all our hard work worth the effort.

With our feet back on solid ground, we continued to try to place all of the pieces of our puzzle in the proper order, and get rid of all of the round pegs and square holes. One theory that was pounced upon made all of the pieces fall into place. (Thank You Crime Lab)

Since the location where the attack on Macdonald, as described by him, occurred was completely discounted due to the lack of pajama threads on the floor where the shirt was reported to have been torn asunder, and the top heavy coffee table being set up so nice and neatly on top of the Esquire magazine (Manson Murders) We took the initial confrontation to a location where most domestic arguments start, The Master bedroom. We knew that Collete had attended class at the University extension on Ft Bragg during which she shared with the class the problem they were having with one of the children wetting the bed. She was going to bring it up with her husband who differed in opinion about how to handle it internally. What happened and what was discussed in the Macdonald household that night will probably never be known, but one thing we know is that Kimmy, the bed wetter, had gone to bed in the master bed that night, and had wet on Macdonald's side. This could have enflamed Macdonald's, evil temper and kicked off the fatal encounter. We also know from the autopsy and it's extensive review by the Armed forces Institute of Pathology (AFIP) in The Walter Reed Army Medical Center in Washington, DC that the first blow to Colette was probably a fist to the mouth which caused her to bleed. This was either just before or just after she struck him on the forehead with a hairbrush, which caused him to have a reddening of his forehead that was gone by mid-morning. Colette, then in a defensive mode may have stabbed him with a paring knife that was handy, which made him grab the 2X2 wooden club that was part of a closet shelving project that was ongoing, and while fending her off of him since she had the knife, struck her on the upper chest with the club leaving a clear impression of the end of the club on her bruised chest. Somehow in all of this action, Kimmy who has been awakened by the argument, tries to intervene in the middle of the assault, cries out the words "Daddy, Daddy, Daddy, and is struck on the side of her head by Macdonald using the club, This blow renders her unconscious, knocking her to the floor in the bedroom doorway where she bleeds extensively onto the carpeting. Now the incident is at its apex, and Macdonald continues to beat his wife with the club, breaking both of her arms, and caused near fatal injuries to her head and face. It is perhaps during this phase of the attack that his pajama shirt is ripped by Collete, with the pocket falling on to the bedroom floor before it could be stained by her direct bleeding. We now have two unconscious people in this house, and a panicking husband trying to sort out what to do about it.

First he rips the bedding from the bed in the room, and wraps the body of Kimmy in it, and carries her into her bedroom, and places her in her bed. About this time Collete probably regains consciousness and knowing what has transpired, tries to get to Krissy to protect her. She enters the room and is once again confronted by her husband who still has the club. She throws herself across Krissy and is struck even more by the bloody club being wielded by her husband, which sprays blood on the walls and knocks her across Krissy, where she bleeds directly onto the top sheet on her bed. Things have gone much too far and now we need to have damage control, and set up a story. He then took the Bedding in which he carried Kimmy, and wrapped Collete in it, and carries her back into the master bedroom, laying her on the floor. It is during one of these transports that while wearing the bloody shirt, he leaves the bloody impression of the pajama shirt sleeve on the bed sheet.

The die is cast, and he must now sort out and set up the scene to make it look like intruders did it. For now he has the two females either dead or dying. The death of Krissy is now a must because she, as young as she was (3 yrs old) could always say that daddy hit mommy, and he would be cooked., and he lays her back on the bed, and stabs her in the chest, and then pulls her over his lap and off of the side of the bed and stabs her again on the upper back with one of the paring knives he has obtained from the kitchen. He also stabs her with the ice pick, but there are no rage filled stabs, instead he barely pricks her skin in an "S" pattern. He then places her back in bed in a manner that suggests that she was killed in her sleep also. Somehow during all of this he visits the living room where he refers to the Esquire Magazine for particulars about the recent Manson Cult murders. While doing this he leaves the bloody finger smudge on the edge of the magazine page. The final cleanup is then to place weapons from the intruders in a place where they will be found outside of the house, write the word PIG on the headboard in blood, Notify the police and just wait.

This is a short version of what was presented to the jury in Federal Court in Raleigh, NC during that summer trial.

The prosecutors, one of whom was a former JAG captain at CID Headquarters in Washington,DC, Brian Murtagh, and the other the US Attorney for the eastern District of NC did a masterful job of presenting the case for the judge and jury so much better than I have just done. But to prove that justice sometimes does triumph, Macdonald was convicted of two counts of second degree murder, and one count of first degree murder of the baby, Krissy. Maybe her soul will rest a little easier because of the legal team that placed her killer in prison for the rest of his natural life.

Macdonald has filed appeals ever since he was first locked up in Terminal Island, Ca, the last being in Sep 2012, to include trips to the Supreme Court (SCOTUS) all of which were denied. The justices wrote on one of the last appeals that Macdonald's appeals were becoming frivolous. I'm sure he will be there till he rots.The latest of the evidentiary hearings was held in September 2012. In it he made more claims such as a US Marshal was alleged to have made a statement that while he was transporting Helene S. from a small southern Jail to the jail and courtroom in Raliegh, NC she confessed to him that she had participated in the murders. This and all of the other allegations were proved to the court to be untrue, and the judge wrote in his opinion that he had failed to adequately establish the merits of his claims. This is where the case stands as of this writing. His newest wife must be getting lonely. Yes, he was married while incarcerated and moved to a comfortable prison in Maryland, but alone is still alone, and well deserved it is.

This case, as stated earlier, has been a career case for me, running from 17 February 1970 until the end of October 2012. It is permanently engraved in my mind, and I'm sure will stay with me forever.

The Macdonald family living room of 544 Castle Drive, Ft Bragg, NC

Master bedroom crime scene photo

Headboard on Macdonald master bedroom "PIG" is written in wife's blood

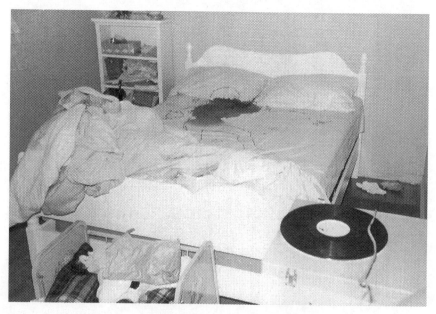

Crime scene photo of the older child's bed

Crime scene photo of younger child's bed

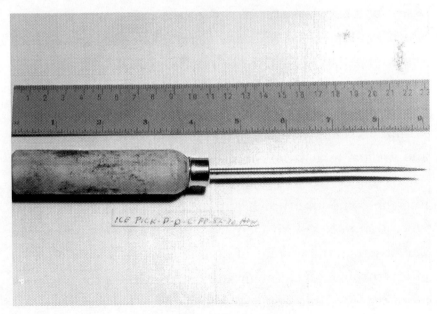

The ice pick used in the murders

DANANG

I thought that a tour of duty in Vietnam might slow me down and allow me to assume a more sedate existence in CID. When I landed in Danang, I learned that the only thing that changed was the geography. Since I was traveling in civilian clothing and not in uniform, I had more freedom of movement since no one had any idea of how I should be treated. I approached one of the soldiers who were in-processing my flight into the country, and asked for a telephone. I called the local CID covert drug team which was known as JNID, or the Joint Narcotics Investigation Division. I had obtained the number from a former JNID Team Chief who was trying to get me assigned to the unit. He told me to sit tight and someone would contact me shortly. Within an hour I was collected by some scruffy looking guys and spirited away from the in processing unit at the Danang Air Base. They drove me into the bowels of Danang City and into the compound which was the Safe House for the JNID Operation in Northern Vietnam. There I met with others who were assigned there, some of whom I knew from previous CID offices throughout Germany and the US. One of the guys took me on a guided tour of the site which was an old, but still intact, Three story former French Government building. I was told that when not on an assignment, they lived in the safe house, which was pretty well protected from attack by the ever present Viet Cong Guerillas. On each floor there was an M-60 machine gun, an M-16 or a tommy gun at each window, and on the roof 2 more machine guns and boxes of ammunition. In the event of an attack on the facility everyone had an assigned defensive position to man. I was given a position on the 2d floor. It was the time of the annual Tet holiday when the Vietcong, and the North Vietnamese Army stirred up trouble for the allied forces in the country the most notable being the Tet Offensive of 1968 which, although the offensive was won by the US Forces, it changed the way the US government viewed US involvement. In one of the rooms in the Safe house there was a five drawer security safe. When it was opened by the Chief, I saw that each drawer was filled to capacity with all sorts of handguns. I was told to select one since we were going out on the town that night. I picked an old favorite of mine which was a 9mm Browning Hi-power pistol. Why this one? I had previously fired one and I liked the way it felt. Being so armed, I felt like I was ready to meet Vietnam. That evening 4 or 5 of us American CID agents, accompanied by 3 Vietnamese civilian policemen, climbed into what was described to me as covert JNID vehicles (Black Jeeps) and headed to a French restaurant for dinner and subsequently on to a Vietnamese night club.

The club was dark, with only a few customers, and was definetly not your typical neighborhood bar. We all sat at the bar and were immediately surrounded by some of the local hookers. I was told not to pay attention to them and stay with the group. That sounded like sound advice. There was one of the hookers who sat next to me and started pestering me to by her a Saigon tea. Not knowing what this was, convinced me to say no, which I did for about ½ half hour. When it came time for us to leave, the chief called for the bill from the bartender. When he looked at it he showed it to one of the Vietnamese cops who were sitting with us, and he started laughing. It seemed that every time someone ordered a drink, he also put down Saigon tea for each of the hookers sitting at the bar. The total was astronomical. When the bartender was told where he could put the bill, he got upset and signaled to someone in the club. One of the CID Agents then said, "Oh Shit, Here we go." At about that time, two men came out of the back of the club, each holding a US Carbine and running for the front of the club by the exit. One grabbed a steel security grate, and tried to slam it closed, locking us in. One of our guys beat him to it and cold-cocked him with ball bearing filled slap stick. We then began to exit the club. Then from inside we heard gunshots ringing out and we then returned to make sure everybody with us was OK. All of our guys had their hands filled with guns, and not wanting to feel left out I drew my Browning and joined the gang in returning fire on the Vietnamese from the back of the club. We hosed down the club, and I was reaching for my second 15 round magazine when the verbal signal was made to "UN ASS" this place, which we did. The Vietnamese cops said "No Sweat lets go." This was a term I learned quickly, was the signal to get our collective ass out of Dodge.

When we returned to the safe house, the Vietnamese cops said that the guys in the back were probably VC, and that the military had been watching the place for a few months. .

It was a nice time to learn this little tidbit. There was never a report of a shooting that came out of that club.

I stayed with the JNID crew for about a week before a flight was available for me to travel south to Saigon.

I arrived at the Danang Air Base to catch my flight and was told that the C-130 cargo plane on the tarmac was to be my link back to reality. There was what looked like a plane load of men waiting for this same flight. As we loaded I noticed that there were some Green Berets also on the flight and that they were maneuvering themselves along the planes bulkhead. I took this to be good advise and followed suit.

There were no seats on the plane, not even the familiar webbing seats usually found on C-130s. We were told to place our luggage by our feet and to remain standing. The plane was so full that with everyone standing, there was no room to move. That's the way we remained throughout the take off and then again at landing. During the flight we could sit on our bags. About 1 ½ hrs later we landed at Bien Hoa which was just north of Saigon. I was collected again by members of the CID and was given billeting at what was known as the monkey Hau. So called, because at one time in the past, monkeys from the nearby jungle had taken over the building, and had held off humans from retaking the building till a group of exterminators had run them off. I had a cozy little room which was just big enough for me, my bed, a refrigerator, and a small bedside table. I was told this was first class accommodations for Vietnam.

- The next day I reported to the CID Headquarters in Long Binh which was a super large supply depot that the VC liked to bombard with mortars, rockets and small arms fire. I was to be assigned to the Crime Suppression team that worked monumental fraud cases from the port of

Saigon. People were stealing millions of dollars worth of vehicles and supplies daily from this port. Sounded like a soft assignment: "WRONG" As I was being assimilated into the group, I met with the CID people there and found others who I had met in the States. They were a great bunch of guys with whom who I still have contact. Having been there for a number of weeks, I was told that the overall Commander of the CID in Saigon for whom I had worked on the Macdonald murder case, wanted to see me ASAP in Saigon. He even had a small plane that he sent up for me. I packed a bag and flew off to the big city. To say that the Colonel Commanding CID Officer in Vietnam was a great guy is a gross understatement. This was the finest man, Colonel or not, that I had ever had the honor to meet and work for. He was, and still is a fine Gentleman who should have long ago been promoted to General Officer.

Col Jack told me that he knew I wanted to be assigned to JNID, but that JNID was about to be closed down and phased out of the CID Group. But he had other plans for me that better fit my qualifications. He offered me the position of Chief of the Criminal Intelligence Division which was here in Saigon. When I researched JNID prior to coming to Vietnam I learned that this was a prestigious, and hardworking position. I readily agreed and finally settled in after a few road trips to Long Binh and back to aquire all of my property. The job also included a civilianized Jeep for transportation. One of the first tasks that I got in this position was to travel to the remote northern town of Qui Nhon which was just south of the infamous Hai Van mountain pass that the VC and NVA were constantly attacking. So much for a quiet vacation on a nice sandy beach. The task at Qui Nhon was to look into allegations that drug evidence which had been collected over a number of years, had not been properly safeguarded by the CID Evidence Custodian. I started the inquiry by conducting a complete inventory of all the evidence being maintained in the Evidence Room. Both the drugs and the documents pertaining to it were years old, and it was evident that there hadn't been any destruction of unneeded evidence for a very, very long time.

This may be a good time to step aside and tell of the atmosphere that was prevalent at this location. Drugs were everywhere one could look. It was not uncommon to see a soldier, or even a group of soldiers waking along the roadways of on the base who looked to be completely zonked out on drugs, and barely able to walk. On top of this was the status of the enemy forces who were the VC and NVA.

They apparently had the run of the place since the base was constantly under attack by rockets and mortars, followed by ground attacks on the fence line The CID office was positioned near the fence line next to the MP barracks, and they had a V-100 armored vehicle parked between the two buildings, next to a large bunker type structure which was the CID defensive position during an attack. Across the street was a set of single story lodging buildings where the CID Agents lived. There were three Agents, one local National interpreter, and local clerk typist assigned to the office. The early warning system for the office and the base as a whole was to watch for the local employees to show up for work. Then everyone knew that there would not be an attack that day. Fool proof Huh? Well, it worked up until I arrived, and on that normal work day when everyone was at work, the mortars began to fall on the base. Then everyone was trained to fall to the floor and get under any desk or bed that was available until the barrage stopped. Then it was a foot race to the defensive position before the ground attack began. Fool proof right?? NOT EVEN. Phase one went ok with the diving and rolling under cover, then phase two went south with people up and running for their defensive position to repel all borders. At this time the mortar barrage started again and the small arms fire started coming from the outside of the perimeter fence. I was among those caught running for the safety of their defensive bunkers, I caught a round from a rifle in my right bicep, and shrapnel in my back from whatever was coming from the rear. It destroyed a jeep that I had just passed and caught me in the left side of my back. I vividly remember seeing my carbine, which I was carrying in my right hand, flying into the air after I was hit. A CID informant, who was at the office, came running to me as I lay on the ground. He had a dirty rag in his hand which he wrapped around my right arm to stop the bleeding. The next I remember is being inside of the bunker with the office Chief hovering over me. He called the MP Company and arranged for the V-100 to take me to the base aid station. That was a wild ride. Once there I was placed on the floor since there were more casualties there. I was looked at by a doctor who had me lay down on the floor again. I kept complaining to the CID Agents who flocked to the aid station that my back was still hurting. They sat me up and the chief then said. "He has a hole in his back". I guess that jacked up the urgency of my condition and I was placed on a guerney and wheeled out to a dust-off chopper and evacuated to the hospital in not too distant Pleiku. The hospital must have been having a bad day, because when we arrived there were not enough guerneys to carry the more seriously wounded into the hospital. I grabbed a man who was badly hurt in his leg, and assisted him in getting into the facility where we all were triaged, and sent to surgery. I returned to Qui Nhon several months later and when I saw the damage to the jeep I had been near when hit, and from that moment felt very lucky to be alive.

I spent 2 weeks in the Pleiku Evac hospital, and then was flown back to Saigon in a 2 engine aircraft which was arranged by Col Jack. The two weeks I spent there were not without incident however, The VC in the surrounding area had a nasty habit of shelling the base at least once daily with 122mm rockets or light mortars in attempts to hit the hospital, You could almost set your watch by the early shelling. With the landing of the first shell, helicopters took off from the nearby airfield LZ and went hunting for the VC launch points. The hospital crews sprang into action and relocated all of the non-ambulatory patients under the ward beds. After a week it just became another nap location. But, they kept trying. A row of beds away from me there was an open space on the floor which was taken up by a Vietnamese family. And I do mean family. During an earlier shelling of a nearby village, a little girl had been wounded, and evacuated to the hospital for treatment. And, of course the entire family came with her and were sleeping on the floor around her bed. It looked like everything the family owned was with them with the exception of chickens and goats. But that is another Air America story. Have you ever flown in an aircraft where meals were cooked on the floor of the plane after the chicken had been beheaded and plucked just before cooking?? That's Air America's in- flight meals.

Two weeks was about all I could take in Pleiku, and I was feeling much better and wanting to get back to Saigon. One call to the CID HQs there and I was on my way in another aircraft waylayed by Col Jack. The next two weeks of recouping was done at the Monkey Hau in Long Binh, with daily trips to the more modern hospital there. John Mays, another Agent,had the pleasure of pouring antiseptic on my wounds daily while he was recouping from some surgery he had gone through the week before. We made it through and then celebrated with a home cooked spaghetti and wine meal which was cooked by the other Agents living in the same quarters. It was very tasty. During my return to Saigon some time later, I had a meeting with Col Jack who felt guilty that he had sent me to Qui Nhon on that mission and he asked me if I wanted to go back to the states. I thought about it and also thought about the fact that if I did go back, I would probably be right back here in about 6 months to complete my tour. I told him that I would rather just stay and get this tour out of the way. And back to work it was. The Criminal Intelligence business in Vietnam covered all of Vietnam, Hong Cong, Thailand, and all points in between. The only place I didn't travel to was Hong Cong. The intelligence gathered by CID in Vietnam was usually tactically important to the fighting troops as well as to the CID, and the paperwork was never ending. We received countless requests for investigative action from all over the world, and each lead received at my office on Yen Do St in Saigon had to be worked. When JNID was in full swing there, the place was usually rocking with activity, but now with the war winding down, the place was quiet. There were two Agents who lived there in the complex which at one time was the main safehouse for the drug operation, but now was but a safehouse for a collection of intelligence files.

We at the Saigon office received a request for action on a case from Ft Bragg which DEA had named "Operation Eagle" which was a massive collection effort to bring down one of the major heroin smuggling and trafficking groups in the US, which had been identified as being headquartered in North Carolina. I remembered this gang from my time at Bragg. The DEA and CID were trying to tie them into the alleged smuggling of heroin from Vietnam to the States in the corpses of deceased soldiers. After working that lead and responding to CID Headquarters in Washington, DC, I decided to look further into it from the Saigon Intelligence Office by conducting an intelligence assessment of that location. I went to the Mortuary on Ton San Nhut Air Base, which is the main mortuary in Vietnam and through which all remains were prepared and shipped to the States. I spent a couple of weeks there looking into the operation, and had the opportunity to see their procedures in action from the receiving of the bodies thru the preparation of them for shipment and the final packing of the bodies into the transfer cases and finally onto the planes which carried them to the Philippines and ultimately to the United States. There were opportunities which I documented where it would be easy to insert several kilos of heroin into the transfer cases with no other persons in Saigon being the wiser. On my last scheduled day at the mortuary I was shocked to observe a Staff Sergeant who I had met at Ft Bragg, was there at the Vietnam mortuary. He had been a suspect who had been ousted by the CID DEA Task Force for heroin involvement, and he told me that he was a part time employee of a local Fayetteville funeral home. BINGO!!!

When they got this information from CID HQs in Washington, DC I hear that the DEA folks were extremely happy. That was one for the good guys.

The rest of my tour was relatively uneventful. When asked, I extended my tour until the treaty deadline for all US Forces to be out of country. I was able to witness the destruction of numerous aircraft that were to be left on the flight line, and strange unexplained fires in buildings that were also to be turned over to the NVA. It wasn't much in the entire scheme of things but it made one feel good. When the peacekeeping forces began arriving in Saigon in accordance with the Paris Peace agreement, I made contact with the Canadian Princess Patricia's Infantry folks who were preparing to go out into the jungle to make verifications that all US Forces were leaving the country. According to the treaty, they were all unarmed. I warned them not to go out there without weapons, but they said that they would be fine. After a few week s some of them came back and reported that they had been attacked at several locations by both VC and NVA and had several of their troops wounded. When I again offered them weapons, they readily accepted. I had quite a collection of firearms and ammo that I had salted away, and that night I and a Canadian Major loaded them into a jeep, and they disappeared. In their place I found several bottles of Canadian whiskey which I shared with the remnants of the US CID and the Canadians. What a night. One of the weapons I gave them was a 12 gauge shotgun with a case of ammo. I'm sure they made good use of all the guns. They had learned the hard way not to trust the enemy.

During my final trip to Camp Alpha, the Vietnam replacement station, I was one of the last CID Agents counted by the NVA as we left. As my plane took off I looked down at the city thinking about the few Agents who remained under Embassy cover that finally escaped from the country in 1975 through the US Embassy/helicopter evacuation.

The extension I made to stay till the end paid off in an assignment which was the best of the best.

The last known combat casualty being MEDEVACED to Saigon Army Hospital

The last known combat casualty being MEDEVACED to Saigon Army Hospital

The last known combat casualty being MEDEVACED to Saigon Army Hospital

Author in front of CID HQs in Long Binh

Monkey Hau CID Billets

Well armed author in Billets in Long Binh

Author standing at location where 2 days later he would be shot and wounded

LEVEL ONE

~⊚~

The Army CID attacked the drug war in three levels. Level Three was the responsibility of the local Detachments at the various Army installations around the world. It dealt with GIs and civilians who were in possession of one or more of the drug categories identified by the Drug Enforcement Agency, or DEA, for personal use. The complaints at this level were usually from Army unit commanders who found drugs during an inspection, or unit level urinalysis, or suspected one or more of his soldiers of abusing illegal drugs, including prescription drugs. These Cases were referred to the local CID office which sent the suspected drugs off to the CID laboratory for testing and confirmation, and, depending on the lab results, the CID would then prepare an investigative report which the commander would use in preparing courts martial charges against the soldier(s) if warranted.

Level Two dealt with drug possession and use at a slightly higher level, and were usually handled at Field Office or District level in a more structured manner. At this level locally assigned soldiers who were dealing drugs were targeted by a drug suppression team from the higher office. The CID Agents at this level occasionally worked in a semi-covert status when authorized by the local CID Commander. The amounts, and types of drugs were usually connected to a drug source. At this level coordination was maintained with the drug suppression team of the higher CID headquarters. The quantities of drugs at this level ran into the ounce levels.

The billy badass of the drug suppression teams is the Level One team, which until recently was situated at the Headquarters of the Second Region of the CID Command in the Heidelberg/ Mannheim area of Germany. It was the team which was set up in the mid 1960s in Mannheim to which my old friend "Ace" was assigned. It was the sole Level One Drug Suppression Team in the entire Army, and was a highly sought after assignment. The team, composed of experienced CID Agents, German investigators assigned to the 2d Region, Professional informants, and some military police investigators who were prospects for full time assignment to the CID. The entire team was headed by a highly experienced senior warrant officer who was also the commander of the Level One Fraud Team, both of which were assigned to the Investigations Branch of the 2d CID Region Headquarters. The Investigations Branch, and the Level One teams, answered only to the 2d Region Commander who was a senior Colonel destined to be a General Officer. The Drug Suppression Team, (DST) was a deep cover operation. In that each Agent was assigned to a geographic area of Germany, and actually lived in one of the large metropolitan areas in Germany, Holland, and other countries where they were needed. They worked in a completely covert manner, having established new and solid cover identities complete with the necessary documentation such as passports, German drivers licenses, and other required ID. They fully immersed themselves into the drug culture of each location, and only surfaced for covert operational meetings once a month, or whenever a meeting was required for operational reasons. In short, a completely undercover operation. Each covert Agent worked primarily with the covert drug operation, of the regional German police, both at the Federal and State levels. . The mission of the DST was to Target international drug traffickers and/or terrorists either alone or with a team of trustworthy informants, or German police Agents. They would establish themselves as US ex-patriots who were in the drug business, and negotiate with the bad guys for delivery of large quantities of drugs, weapons, explosives or whatever the bad guys were dealing with. The quantities of drugs involved in the deals started at 50 kilos of hashish, 100 kilos of weed marijuana, 5 kilos of heroin or cocaine, or in one case 1 million hits of LSD. If they had any lesser amounts they were identified and referred to the local CID offices and their level two DST through overt means. No physical contact was allowed between level one agents and level two operations. During the last 20 or so years of operation, international terrorist operations, which were rampant in Europe were included in the targeting of the Level One DST. At the Investigations Branch level, liaison was maintained with CIA, DEA, and the US Consulate in Frankfurt. This was a rocky road since DEA, which had a small office in the consulate, was not allowed to work drug investigations overtly in Germany based upon the Status of Forces Agreement between the German Government and the US State Dept. They could only report on drug intelligence which the Level one and two teams developed. They were completely dependent upon the CID to accomplish this mission. They however were allowed to use paid DEA informants in some cases. In order to obtain reliable informants, the DEA agents would use their deep pockets to try to recruit informants we had registered with the CIA source registry. But, for the most part we enjoyed a good working relationship with DEA and worked some high level cases with their help. Especially when dealing with organized US criminal groups.

Now that that stage has been set, allow me to bring myself into the picture. My choice assignment after extending my time in Vietnam was to the Headquarters of Second Region in Heidelberg which oversaw all criminal investigative activity in Europe. . When I arrived there I met with several Agents with whom I had been stationed in Vietnam and also at Ft Bragg. I was initially assigned as the Agent in Charge of the intelligence branch, and settled down to a routine of reviewing CID And other Police agency reports and extracting intelligence, and developing intelligence gathered during my trips through Europe, which I then passed to the responsible CID office either in Europe or world-wide.

It was during this period that I was selected to attend the prestigious Senior Detective course at Scotland Yard in London for two months. While there I made some great and lasting friendships which served me well while working on a large cocaine case in Stuttgart, Germany

Being collocated with the DST, made it just a matter of time until I was introduced to the world of the Level One. I worked jointly on a number of Intelligence cases, and formed close relations and friendships with the covert side of the picture. The Chief of the investigations Branch and the Level One DST, was a man I had relieved in Vietnam, and had the greatest respect for. Gary P. was a part of the JNID in Saigon, and was also the

Chief of Intelligence there. We had many stories between us, and were personal friends. He asked me one day if I would assist the DST in a case that needed a fresh face to deliver a briefcase filled with German money, which was flash money for a major drug deal in Frankfurt. I jumped at the opportunity. A meeting had been set at a very nice Italian restaurant not far from the US Consulate. I arrived in a taxi, and when I entered I saw GLP sitting with two Turkish men who looked a little on the rough side. I joined them, and then passed the briefcase to GP who cracked it open just enough to see the money. The men he was dealing with, were getting nervous and their eyes never stopped roving over the entire restaurant. Then speaking in the German language to the two Turks, he told them the money was here and he wanted to see the heroin that had been negotiated for. Apparently there was another meeting site set up, because one of the Turks called a number on his cell phone, spoke in Turkish, and then passed the phone to GP who then spoke again in German for a short time and then returned the phone to the Turk, who apparently said that he had the money. The phone went back to GLP who spoke in English to one of his DST Agents on the other end of the line. Then from the bowels of the restaurant 5 men in waiters uniforms converged on our table. One was carrying what looked like An MP-5 sub-machinegun, and was pointing it menacingly at our table. The others grabbed the two Turks and hustled them out of the restaurant onto the street and into a non-descript van. GLP then took his glass of wine from the table, raised it and said that other members of the team on the other end of the phone, had the heroin, were also greeted by a German apprehension team, and the Turks on their end were also on the way to another van. We finished our wine, and then GP and I headed for a meeting with the German police at another location. It was there I leaned that the flash money was the property of the German Police and they were anxious to get it back. The folks on the other end of the phone had been one DST CID Agent, and one of his informants. The heroin was also in the custody of the German police, and everyone was happy. The location we met was a wine bar with a very nice garden. We debriefed there, shared a few bottles of wine while doing so and then headed back to the office. That was my introduction to covert activity at this level, and it was cool. Back at the office he asked me if I was interested in coming on board as his deputy since the incumbent was rotating back to the US to retire. I warned him that the Lieutenant Colonel I worked for at the Intel office would have a baby if he found out. GP said that would not be a problem since he had already approached the commander with the idea and had received the nod. The LTC, as predicted, almost had a coronary attack when he found out. We went toe to toe over it with him claiming that he had been taken advantage of while he was on vacation and that he had me sent to the Scotland Yard Senior Detective course and that he felt betrayed. We never had a great relationship anyway, so I didn't feel bad.

Depicts Special Agent Bill Ivory coordinating a major drug deal

Depicts Special Agent Bill Ivory, in front of Heidelberg/
Seckenheim Germany CID HQs

Author sitting in front of the Level One Seizure board

GLP, and team secretary counting out $500,000.00 in flash money before a
major cocaine seizure in Stuttgart, Germany

A monthly meeting of German State Police Agents and CID Level One Agents

The staff of the Investigations Branch of the German CID Region

114

6 Kilos of high grade heroin seized by Level One Agent in Stuttgart, Germany

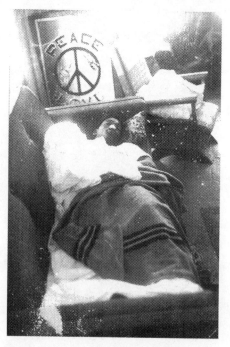

Victim of tainted heroin seized near Wuerzburg, Germany

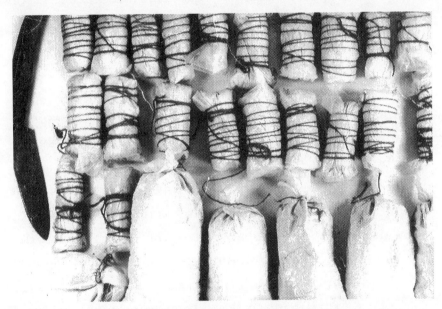

5 Kilos of high grade heroin which caused the deaths
of both American and German drug users.

THE INTERNATIONAL CONNECTION

<hr>

$\mathcal{A}\copyright$ $\copyright\mathcal{A}$

The daily routine at the DST office was filled with administrative paperwork such as reviewing reports from the agents in the field which contained details of all covert contacts made by them, the records of all covert funds expended during each investigation, which was a full time job in itself, and in general, keeping an eye on all of the undercover activities of all of the agents. Occasionally the agents, working with the German police agencies would need some US currency to cement a deal pending with traffickers, and I would arrange for the local Army finance office to provide the amount needed which would then be "flashed" to the drug traffickers to show our bonafides to them. When necessary I would carry the funds to the field and take part in the flash operation, and depending on the amount of the flash, ascertain if the German side of our operation had the location covered to prevent a rip off, or an attempt to steal the funds which ranged from $50,000. to $500,000 per operation. We did this whenever US currency was needed since the German authorities had a very hard time getting large amounts of used dollar bills, and conversely, the

German were always ready to provide the necessary amounts
of German currency needed for a deal. The security they
provided for the currency being used was outstanding. Both the
Federal and State police had undercover units that performed
covert surveillance of both undercover drug operations, and
terrorist operations that were virtually invisible with their agents
capable of completely merging with the general population.
One such operation which required a $500,000 US Dollar flash
was the first major cocaine deal encountered in Europe. The
deal started when one of the paid informants working for us
approached his agent handler with information that there were
a number of Columbian males who were hitting the nightclub
scene in Frankfurt, and making contact with people there who
were involved in the drug trade, looking for a solid contact for
large quantities of cocaine that they could have delivered to
Germany from Columbia. This was something that got a lot of
blood pressures raging since the largest cocaine seizure to date
in Germany was only in the ounce amounts, and most were from
stocks of legitimate cocaine in hospital and dental sources. The
informant was told to make contact with these South Americans,
and attempt to set up a meeting with them to discuss business
arrangements. The Hessen State Police and German Customs in
Frankfurt were in complete disbelief of the individuals involved.
When we approached the Baden-Wuerttemburg State Police in
Stuttgart they were as excited about the possibility that this could
happen as we were. Contact was established with the purported
cocaine dealers, and negotiations began. It was a long road
that took us to many of the large cities in Germany, and one
city in another, unnamed country, which will not be identified
here for political reasons. It took us almost exactly one year

to reach a mutually agreeable price and location for delivery of the drugs. The South Americans were part of a Columbian Cartel which was attempting to open long term opportunities in the European drug scene. The final negotiations were held in the nightclub scene in Stuttgart which featured very classy strippers, and was definitely not, a second rate operation. The strippers were a part of an international syndicate which kept the dancers travelling on a monthly schedule to the higher class of nightclubs throughout Europe. We met with the Columbians at several of the clubs and established to them that we did have the kind of money that they were looking for. We established ourselves as American heroin traffickers who had the ability to successfully smuggle large quantities of heroin from Europe to the United States. This impressed the South Americans to the extent that they had a sizeable quantity of their cocaine sent to Stuttgart for us to have as a sample of their wares. The night they turned this sample over to us, they were acting very proud of their ability to provide a high grade of cocaine for our business. The turnover was held in a very high end restaurant in Stuttgart which, at a much later date, was bought by a very popular formula one race car driver who was absolutely not involved in any of drug trafficking we were initiating there. The meal was great, washed down by a number of bottles of fine wine, GLP being a wine connoisseur who had an envious collection of fine Italian wines at his home. The bill at the end of the evening was staggering, but out came my wallet filled with our confidential funds. The Columbians were dutifully impressed. At the time, I owned a Corvette that had legal German registration in my covert name. GLP and I used this two seater on a number of occasions to impress the various traffickers we were dealing with at the time. We were using it for this deal to limit the number of people we could transport at any given time. We didn't want the Columbians to be able to be with us in a car when the time came for any money flash that hopefully would occur. The German State police were having orgasms over the deal at this point, and when we turned the cocaine sample over to Max, who was the chief of the covert drug team, who was a Kriminal Haupt-Kommisar, the equivalant to a US Police Detective Captain, He declared that a celebration was in order. We went to a bar on top of one of Stuttgart's finest hotels. The bar was co-located with the hotel's swimming pool and sauna, and was a great place to relax and unwind from the day's work. While relaxing we debriefed what had occurred in the restaurant, and plans were initiated to locate a suitable place for the deal to go down. We were that satisfied that the deal would happen. As the hours and drinks passed, we began to interact with some of the other hotel guests who were there to enjoy the bar and the spa facilities of the hotel. Now the sauna was a typical German sauna, in that it was textile-frei, meaning that no clothing or bathing suits were allowed in the sauna for health reasons. This is universal throughout Europe. Europeans who use saunas are very particular about the protocol, and will defend it fiercely. They will sit in the sauna for a certain period, and then exit, shower, and if available jump into a cool swimming pool to refresh themselves and then repeat the ritual until it's time to go home.

The other patrons were a mixed bunch of male/female residents of the hotel with ages ranging from mid 20s to late 50s. The consumed alcohol notwithstanding, they were an attractive bunch. When we were invited to join them in the Spa, naturally we were happy to oblige. There were 8 or 10 of us, including two female State Police Agents, and we hid our pistols in lockers with our clothing and joined the festivities. Once in a sauna, there are no secrets that can be kept from anyone. We made several circuits of the sauna to pool and return, and were having a great time with more than a little groping going on. One of the more junior German agents was assigned the duty of transporting the cocaine sample obtained earlier, minus a small amount we, the US agents, kept to be sent to our laboratory for analysis and maintained for signature purposes in the event someone else encountered some from the same point of manufacture, we would all be notified., This is common practice among police agencies world-wide. Our portion was then taken by me, to a room we had rented, and was locked in the room safe. When we closed the bar, much later than its normal closing time, the party bunch all went their separate ways. When we next met with them at the hotel's breakfast, it was hard to imagine that just a few hours earlier, we had all been naked at the bar. There were a few I didn't recognize at first with their clothes on. Chalk up another experience.

We maintained contact with the brothers, meeting in different cities and countries to cement our reputation as high level drug dealers. As our meetings progressed, the information began to flow more easily, and we learned that the uncle was a high ranking member of the Bogota Cartel who was a very cautious person. He wanted to be sure that we were not connected to any police organization. Part of this caution was put to ease when the brothers were not arrested when they handed over the sample. As we continued to meet, we decided to meet in a city in a neighboring country. When we met we took them to one of the syndicated nightclubs where we knew some of the dancers from Stuttgart would be working. The brothers were duly impressed, and when we fixed them up with two Filipino girls who we knew, they were amazed. When we finally met with the uncle, he mentioned that the brothers had told him about their adventures and were convinced that we were not from the police. Also during this trip we discussed the business that we wanted to conclude, and that we could handle 20 kilos of cocaine the first time and more after that on a monthly basis. The price was also discussed, and agreed upon. Date of delivery was set, and everybody went home happy.

About a month later the informant contacted us and advised that the final business would be conducted within a week. However, for security purposes the uncle would only deal 10 kilos this trip. We went into overdrive then making an operational plan with the Stuttgart State Police, arranging for the flash/buy money in US dollars. The flash was set for a location that the German Police were comfortable with surveilling. After this, the deal would go down in two days. We balked at this and settled for the flash to be followed immediately by the buy. We selected a luxury hotel in downtown Stuttgart, directly across from the Main Train Station, as the location, reserving two rooms, one for us, the other for the deal to happen in. The German Police made their arrangements in the hotel to maintain security over the $500,000 we were bringing in my Corvette. It was also arranged that we would meet with the brothers in the lobby bar at a certain time for the money flash. After that we would meet with the uncle and his nephews in the room rented for them which was bugged and under video surveillance by the Germans, show the money again, which was in a briefcase and when the cocaine was brought out we would signal the German arrest team which would then enter the suite, using a hotel furnished passkey and make the arrests.

The first phase went well in the lobby with the brothers peeking into the full briefcase at the bundles of bills we had in it. We then adjourned to the room upstairs where we met with the uncle who had two large suitcases sitting on the king sized bed. We had a few minutes of small talk and general conversation while getting to meet the uncle. We showed the money again, and the uncle said the cocaine was in the suitcases. He had one of the brothers open a suitcase and begin to peel back the lining. The cocaine had been molded perfectly to fit in the suitcase and not be detected by a visual search. When we saw and handled the cocaine, and were satisfied that it was in fact cocaine, the signal was given and within seconds, the door flew open, and the German version of our SWAT team made a dynamic entry with submachine guns at the ready. One of the brothers made the mistake of diving onto the bed in an attempt to get to a pistol he had hidden under a pillow. Poor naïve lad. He was pounced on by three of the entry team and severely beaten when he resisted. The loaded pistol was one of three found during the post arrest search. They were apparently ready to protect either the uncle or the load of cocaine, or maybe both. I was amazed that the entry team didn't just shoot the Columbian. He gave them all of the justification they needed.

There was a little stir as the Columbians were handcuffed and brought out of the hotel through the delivery entrance, but not very much. It was handled very discreetly for the hotel management.

One would think that this was the end of a well handled deal. Well, not exactly. within weeks of being incarcerated in Germany's high security prison where they put their terrorists like the Bader-Meinhof Gang that had terrified Germany for years. Robbing, killing, and bombing both American and German families and facilities. Our uncle simply walked out of the prison after buying off one or more of the prison personnel. A massive search for him found that he had boarded a freighter in northern Germany and was heading for South America through the English Channel.

Here I put my contacts in Scotland Yard to work. I called one of my mates there and explained the situation asking for assistance. He got right on it and began to narrow the search for the ship. He contacted the maritime police who assisted him as much as they could, but they couldn't stop and search the ship without a search warrant. I obtained what documents I could from the German Police but they didn't arrive in time to get a warrant and grab the guy before the ship cleared into international waters. When asked if they could notify the authorities where the ship was destined they advised that there would be no cooperation from them. In short, uncle had made a good escape thanks to his cartel money. The nephews? They remained in German prison. I think they were happy with that, knowing that if and when they returned to Columbia, a Columbian necktie probably awaited them. There was not much publicity on the escape from Stammheim prison. I'm sure there were some red faces in the prison system over this incident.

Another opportunity arose for me to continue with my law enforcement education and so off I went to attend the Drug Enforcement Administration Course which was held at the DEA

Headquarters at 14ᵗʰ & I Sts in NW Washington, DC. The course was all business and was taught by experienced field agents from the DEA. There were a lot of long days, but at night the students would usually band together and hit the bar and club scene in the DC area. One of the clubs which was convieniently located across I st from the DEA, featured middle eastern dancers, or at least they purported themselves to be. The floor show there was always great entertainment with belly dancers being the headliners. One of the dancers was headlined as "Little Egypt, and what a show she put on. After a few weeks we were all friends and every night she would go into the audience and select a guy to come up on stage and dance with her. She picked me several times and once on stage, we would make a big production out of it. On one particular night, she brought me on stage and we were in the middle of a great dance when I felt something inside my pants starting to move. It was crawling down my pants leg, and it felt like I would be exposing myself in a very short time. But let's back up just a bit. The class all carried our pistols with us since during the first week there at school a couple of the guys and a female officer who was also attending the class were walking across the parking lot next to the DEA building, and were accosted by 2 locals with knives who wanted to rob them. The old saying comes to mind: "Never bring a knife to a gun fight!" and when all three pulled their weapons out, the local bad guys hauled ass out of the parking lot. When this was brought up in class the next day, the instructor very sternly warned us not to travel anywhere in DC without a gun being handy. And after that incident we All complied. Well, back to my leg crawling incident. I was carrying my .38 cal pistol in my waistband with no holster, but had the handle all wrapped in rubber bands which, according to the DEA firearms instructor, would keep the pistol from falling out of the pants waist. Yeah, the pants waist, but mine was sliding down my leg. Luckily for me the tabletops were even with the dance floor, and that we had grabbed three tables right at ringside. I maneuvered myself over towards one of our tables, but the gun wouldn't wait. I called to one of my classmates to be alert, and that was as far as I got, As the pistol slipped to the end of my trouser leg I gave a little kick and the pistol went bouncing across the stage towards the table where my partner, was looking at me like I had lost my mind when I said "Grab the gun". It was a well placed kick and the gun ended up in his lap. This didn't escape the attention of many of the other customers, but Little Egypt's very scant, and well filled costume helped I'm sure, because most of them never saw the artillery change hands. I wore a holster after that.

The drug deals didn't happen every day like you would see on a TV show. We had some dry periods when nothing was moving, and others when it was difficult to keep up. There was one deal with an informant who was hurting for money and wanted to do a deal in Stuttgart and get some bonus money which was paid by us to performing informants. Gary and I met with the informant who was from one of the "Stans" bordering Turkey. He had been active and made some decent deals, but for about 6 months he hadn't turned anything and his funds were cut off. Some of our informants were given a monthly stipend and had their expenses paid by us from our confidential drug funds. These however, were our high performing informants like the one who turned the cocaine deal for us who we had given $2500. The one we met that day in Stuttgart had the contacts and ability to turn deals but he was either too lazy, or unmotivated to work for his money. He had his son with him who was in his early 20s, and who was there to help his dad out. The informant told us when he called that he had a deal for a half kilo of heroin and he could arrange for a sale that day. When he returned to us after unsuccessfully trying to locate the dealer with the dope, He said that his son could contact one of his many drug connections in West Berlin with whom he was also aquainted, and arrange a deal. It was decided that I would accompany him to Berlin, and meet with the dealer there, and make a deal for some heroin. This was prior to us opening a level one office in Berlin, so I had one of our German investigators call to the Berlin police and inform them that I would be arriving shortly in their city and may be calling on them for assistance. Little did I know that there was a World Cup Soccer game being televised that afternoon. We went to the Stuttgart airport, bought two round trip tickets to West Berlin and in an hour we were there. He took me by taxi to a neighborhood of apartment buildings in the north side of town where we went to one and he rang the bell and talked in his Arabic type language to someone over the intercom. In a few minutes a middle-eastern looking man came to the door and spoke with my informant. While this was happening, the man at the door was giving me a real hard looking over with a look that made me happy that I had a 9 mm pistol with me. He finally let us in and escorted us to an upper floor where I again went thru the hard looks by another mid-eastener. When we were let into the apartment I noticed that there were PLO posters and other papers laying on tables. If that wasn't bad enough, there were four other men in the living room who were busy bindling up a small pile of what looked like a pound of heroin into user size packages. To top off the day, another man came into the room and apparently asked the informant in a very harsh manner who I was. . They had a discussion and the man settled down and addressed me in very passable English. We had a long and very interesting conversation about me making a purchase of quantities of heroin from him. He was apologetic about not being able to since the heroin being packaged at the table was destined for a dealer in Berlin, and he wouldn't have more for a few days. We spoke more about future deals and he said he was interested, but not from his house. I made an attempt to smooth our way out of the apartment by inviting him to meet with myself and some others I worked with in Frankfurt in the near future. The manner in which the other four men addressed the late comer made it obvious that he was senior person in that apartment. I then told the informant that we were leaving and he showed relief on his face when he heard that. Once outside I mentally noted the address and apartment numbers and as we walked away from the building the informant said that he was getting very afraid of those men and was glad to be leaving with his head still on. I told him if he ever got me into a situation like that again, I would be the one he should be afraid of. I promised him that I would shoot him in the head and throw his body into the river. Judging from the expression on his face, I think he believed me. We had just left a PLO drug operation that was in full swing. During that period the PLO was a sought after terrorist group responsible for countless kidnappings, bombings and murders. One being the 1972 Olympic terror operation. I immediately started calling our police contacts in Berlin to advise them of what I had seen. At the city police, and customs office there was no response, and at the US Army MP station I learned from the German Police Desk Sgt there that all of the city drug personnel had logged out and could not be reached that day. They were all out at their favorite bar watching the damned soccer game. I dragged the informant back to the airport and we left. The German Police hit the house the next day after being called to Task from the Berlin Police Oberat, or the Police Commissioner. One thing this mini adventure did was to show us we needed a covert presence in the divided city. Berlin was on the main smuggling line from Turkey, through Bulgaria and into Germany. The incoming and outgoing flights had no Customs, or document inspections, and traffic throughout the city on the subway system could not be inspected by anyone due to the treaty signed with Russia after WW11. Someone arriving at the airport with a load of dope could easily transit the city with the subway system and never fear any police or customs inspection. Negotiations were started right away with the Commanding General of the Berlin Command which still wielded a big stick after the war. The General was more than 100% in agreement that we needed the presence of the level one operation, once he was briefed on its capabilities, and record of success. The level one agents in what is called "the Zone" each had covert apartments which they paid for with their travel funds. The Berlin CG told me that when we found a suitable apartment, he would pay for it with his confidential funds, He also introduced me to his property manager and told him to give me anything from his warehouse that I wanted, The Berlin Command issued furnishings to people at the Ambassadorial level, and nothing was too good for them and likewise, us. The agent chosen to open the office was an old Berlin hand, having been stationed there in the good old cold war days. His marching orders were to find a nice apartment, notify the Berlin General's office of the costs involved, and then go furniture shopping for some of the nicer stuff they had in the warehouse. Including Rosenthal China and some real nice furnishings. He found a nice multi-bedroom apartment, and furnished it very smartly. It served us well and provided lodging space for other level one agents who happened to be in the city. The apartment was also exempted from any quarters inspection that the Berlin Brigade made on other rental property. With that taken good care of, we went full swing into operation, and began shortly to make some major seizures there. The CG was very happy with our operation which had a rocky start, a number of years ago when one of the level one agents was in town on a deal and was called by an agency that also has 3 letters in its name and was informed that he was to be at the security office of the Berlin Brigade at a certain time ready to brief someone in Washington, DC on an operation over a secure telephone. To be late for this call was not an option. Our man Ken A. (RIP), was, as usual, running a little tight on his schedule when he attempted to enter the secure area of the Berlin Headquarters. The German gate guard had not been warned of this and when he encountered Ken, dressed like and looking like the reincarnation of buffalo Bill complete with his long blond hair, and buckskin jacket, he refused to call the security office and told Ken to leave the headquarters area. WRONG ANSWER!!!. Ken, noting that minutes were ticking away, jumped from his covert car with German plates, grabbed the armed guard, handcuffed him to the gate house and proceeded into the Brigade HQs and into the security office where he was just in time for his phone call. That caused a little hard feelings for a short while until another general Officer at European HQ in Heidelberg called and smoothed things out. When told about the incident, the Berlin Brigade Commander chuckled.

With our operation firmly entrenched, the drug intelligence began to flow, showing that the city was a major source of heroin from Turkey. With the intel, also came CID reports of major seizures of heroin by our operations with the local police, and customs offices. Ken, and his informants, began in earnest to establish themselves as high level drug buyers, making good contacts in the criminal underworld. Ken called Gary and I, as Gary was clearing out of the office in order to return to the states for his well deserved retirement. Ken advised that he had met with a bar owner in the downtown Kuferstandam district who said he had contacts for drugs in the city but wanted to be paid for his information. This was done without knowledge that Ken was with the CID. Ken was acting as a prospective drug buyer, and the man wanted a finders fee for each contact he made for Ken. Ken told him that he knew of an Italian drug trafficker who was looking for a steady contact. That Italian guy was Gary who spoke almost native Italian with a Tuscan accent. Gary and I traveled to Berlin and were introduced to the bar owner. We talked business for quite a while and then he reached under the bar pulled out an old cigar box and opened it to show us what looked like a giant hand rolled hashish bong. He lit it and we were joined by two other bar customers who grabbed it and took a couple of deep hits on it. He passed it to us and we both took phony drags off of it and told him how good the stuff smelled. This made him happy, and more comfortable with us. He then leaned over the bar in a conspiratorial way whispered to us that one of the two guys who were just with us was from the Berlin Kripo, or criminal Police, showing that he had protection. We met with the bar owner several times in the next two weeks, and then Gary had to pull out in order to leave for the States. I continued with periodic meetings with him and we got deeper into the drug trafficking mode. He told me about his criminal backround and how he was involved in trafficking of stolen art pieces such as antique paintings. He then took me to the second floor of the bar which was his apartment which he shared with his wife who was a very flirty and good looking gal. He showed me a number of paintings which he said had been stolen during WW11 in Berlin and were very valuable. He asked if I were interested in guns and when I said yes he pulled a Winchester lever action rifle from his closet and showed me how smooth the action was. He said that he also had access to other stolen firearms, but only wanted to sell in bulk. During this same period, another covert agent from Munich was in touch with an LSD dealer from Berlin and was negotiating for delivery of 500,000 hits of LSD. If things ran smoothly we were going to put a big dent into the Berlin drug trafficking activities. Ken, in the meantime had been introduced by the bar owner to a heroin dealer who could provide quantities of heroin with a high purity level. In the Wuerzburg and Munich area there had recently been a rise in fatal overdosing from high purity heroin, and there were seizures of heroin in the mid to high 90% levels of purity, some of which was found in the possession of US soldiers some of who after injecting it, never got the needles out of their arms before dying. There was a big push on to get to the source quickly by every agent in Europe. Ken was pursuing his contact in Berlin. The go between was an Italian restaurant owner who offered to make the deal go smoothly for Ken, and

set up an afterhours dinner for Ken, his associates, and his boss
who was due to arrive in Germany in the next few days. I was to
be the Godfather type boss with the hands on the big money.
We met for dinner at the restaurant on a late Friday night, and
were treated to a fine 7 course meal with some of the best wine
I had in Germany. When I mentioned this to the owner, he said
that it was for his very special customers. We dined and talked
future business with the dealer and arranged to take delivery
of a quantity of heroin in Frankfurt the following week. At this
meeting the dealer presented a sample of his wares. And was
flashed German currency which he preferred. With the dinner
meeting finished we all parted our ways and were to meet again
in Frankfurt where the heroin dealer was busted by an alerted
German Customs inspector while carrying a half kilo of heroin
in his luggage. It took another month for the LSD deal to come
through, but it did in Munich. The trip was a success but no home
run. The heroin, while high in purity didn't match the heroin in
the overdose cases which, thank goodness, slowed and stopped
after a short period. We encountered more cases of "hotshot"
Heroin from time to time, one being in and around the city
of Wuerzburg. This bad batch of drugs was killing even more
US soldiers. We had informants working to try and locate the
source, when one of them called and told us that the dealer was a
female Stasi, or an East German Intelligence agent. I instructed
the informants CID Agent Handler to try and develop more info
on this female, and being a good CID Agent who always follows
protocol, I informed the local US Military Intelligence office
of our findings. They in turn notified the Army Headquarters
in Heidelberg, and a newly promoted Captain came to see us
all excited about the possibility of catching an East German

Agent. She told me during our first meeting that she had never caught a spy before. I told her that we would try and work a deal with the east German Agent and get her arrested during a drug transfer. She didn't want to share the credit for the arrest and demanded that we back off and let her Handle it. It would have been relatively easy to lure her into an arrest situation, but she was adamant. We backed off and within days the female dealer, who was identified by the German BND (Germany's CIA) as an intel agent disappeared, never to return. Impatience and ego are a great deal killer.

Another encounter with the Stasi occurred in Berlin. There was a German KRIPO agent who was assigned as liaison with the Berlin CID Office, and sometimes appeared during arrest situations with my guys. He was aware of most of the Level One Agents who came into Berlin from "the Zone" or West Germany, to operate undercover. The BND was working a case on him suspecting him of being a Stasi Agent. The day they were going to Arrest him, He was alerted and fled to East Berlin. This caused some concern, but we were pretty sure he had never been to our safehouse, and had never seen any documents identifying our Agents. We tightened up our act in Berlin considerably after that.

Another notable case which caused me to return to Germany to testify at two trials went down in the port city of Hamburg. Ken A, who had such good luck in setting up his operation in Berlin, was selected to open up an office in Hamburg, based on a request from the Police Commissioner in Hamburg who had heard of our operation from other police chiefs around the country during their regular monthly meetings. We had not had very good liaison with Hamburg, and had heard from our British CID friends that they were not a very friendly sort. A large number of the older residents of the city of Hamburg still hold a serious grudge against the US for the bombings that occurred during WW11, destroying the entire port city, and killing thousands. Ken again called me for assistance with a difficult deal he was working with a Turkish trafficker who promised to deliver 6 kilos of Heroin. When I arrived at the airport he briefed me on what had transpired and the oplan for this deal. I was to hold the flash after showing it to the main dealer. Ken would then travel with the dealer in his car to pick up the heroin, then make a call to me at the hotel we were working out of. I would then pretend to give the money to the 17 year old son of the dealer who would have remained at the hotel which the Police had wired, with me waiting for the signal that the deal should go through. When the call came in I was to verbally give the signal to the German police who would then arrest the son while the father was also being arrested outside of the hotel. Seemed simple enough. After the money was flashed I went to the room with the son and the money, and Ken left with the dealer. Then the deal changed. The father wanted to pick up the drugs and then drive back to the hotel and pick up the money and then give the dope to Ken. Sounds like a rip to me. The German cops were panicking. They didn't want to loose the money or the heroin. When the change came to me I said lets just ride with the original plan. The father picked up the heroin from a nearby bar and drove back towards the hotel. When he made a weird turn away from the planned route, Ken bashed him with his pistol, and being wired, let the cops know this, and they closed in on the car and made the arrest. When I heard the pounding of feet in the hallway, I knew the deal was going down right then and I knocked the son on his butt and opened the door for the cops who ran in and arrested him. It was a simple deal made crazy by a greedy dealer who had been in the business for a long time, and his son who was on his first deal. The agreed upon kilos were found in the car after the Arrests were made. This was the first heroin deal that this German drug section had made in a very long time, and they were impressed at how we handled it and were able to work with the dealer changing plans mid-stream. Sometime after I left Germany a few years later and returned to Texas, being assigned to the Fort Hood CID, I was called back to Hamburg twice for trials on this case against the dealer and his juvenile son. The Hamburg criminal police treated me like royalty when I was there, and reserved a suite for me in the Intercontinental Hotel which was a grand place with a tremendous Spa on the top floor. Memories of the Stuttgart cocaine deal flooded back on me while I was there. The only thing missing was the team.

Shortly after that deal I was called by the German Police from the State of Hesse who had arranged for delivery of a large quantity of Heroin which was to be delivered to the quaint town of Bad Homburg. They needed an American to make the flash, which they would supply, and signal for the arrest team to move in. The deal had been set for an old market area that was in the middle of an old renaissance structure that had a lot of tall columns that resembled roman architecture. To gain access to the location one had to either drive up a steep hill and park and walk in, or climb a very long and steep stairway. It was an excellent location for a deal from the dealer's viewpoint since it would be easy to set up counter surveillance on it with few people. Likewise, it was a good location for the police to set up since there would be a large crowd at the market. The plan was for me to climb the stairs and meet the informant who would introduce me to the dealer. I would flash the money, and the dealer would go and pick up the heroin and bring back to me for the exchange. Another easy deal. Bullshit!!!

I made the climb to the top of the stairs, flashed the dealer, who went to get the goods, and then saw a group of people moving towards the stairs from the market area, as I prepared to signal the arrest team, I turned towards the stairs and saw another group of people at the foot, starting to climb towards me. OH SHIT!! Something was very wrong. As the dealer returned with a package for me the group at the top moved in, and grabbed both me, and the dealer. There was yelling coming from the bottom of the stairs, and the group at the top started pulling out guns which they didn't point at me, but at the group at the bottom. The yelling continued from both ends of the stairs until one of the group at the top fired a round at the group at the bottom. It must have looked like an episode from the Keystone Kops albeit with real bullets flying. One of the group at the top was hit and as he fell I began to recognize what was being screamed from both ends. It was in fact a cops vs cops encounter. As the dust began to clear, recognition started to form between the two groups. It was the Bad Homburg Kripo drug team at the top, where they were supposed to be, and from the bottom came drug agents from the German customs Office in Karlsruhe, a major city to the south. They had received intelligence that there was to be a drug deal at the marketplace and they reacted to it without calling the Bad Homburg Kripo. When the Bad Homburg Kripo was asked if they had coordinated with other police agencies in the area before the deal. The answer was no. They didn't want to share the deal. This was the first drug deal they had been in on in years in this sleepy little town. The Bad Homburg Police agent who was shot was hit in the upper thigh and eventually recovered but never went back to work.

After this adventure, it was back to the office for more admin work, and reflections on how easily a deal can go south, and that we were not indestructible. Just a little common sense goes a long way when planning for a deal that can lead to a confrontation. Liaison is just a phone call away, and can make all of the difference in the world.

About this time we received an early Christmas present from our headquarters in Washington. We were expecting to get some new covert vehicles from the HQs, but were surprised when they were delivered. The new fleet consisted of Fiats and some really nice Opal sedans, One of the Opals which was destined for the Chief's office (Me) was an Opal GTE, a semi sports model of the line which came with a souped up version and a super body design. This was a very pleasant surprise. We also got as a bonus item, a new Fiat van that we were going to convert into a surveillance vehicle which we would control, but make available for use by some of the level 2 drug teams when necessary. We eventually outfitted it with customs seats in the back that would make a long term surveillance lot more comfortable, new side windows fitted with one way glass, a sound system to record what was happening during an operation, and tandem batteries to keep all of the systems running without strain on the main battery. We had one of our German civilians approach a large body shop in Heidelberg that we used to repair our vehicles to set up a cover for the vehicle. We then had magnetic signs made using the cover which were blessed by the shop owner. The bigger surprise was a shipment of covert weapons for use only by our team. The shipment consisted of an S&W 9mm, several Walther P38s which were seized by DEA on some operation stateside, and several Browning high power 9mm. Both the P38s, and the Brownings had old Nazi swastika markings on them which told us they were made during WW11, and were actually collector items. They all had high capacity magazines which make us happy campers. There were also 8 small framed .380 cal pistols which were for back-up weapons in the event of an emergency in the field when a primary weapon was for some reason unavailable to the agent. These palm sized pistols were at first welcomed by the agents, but an incident occurred which had me recall all of them for being unsafe. The incident happened in the Wuerzburg area where the agent with the most experience was assigned. Our agent, Graven, had been working with the Bavarian State Police for years and was very well respected by all on the Bavarian drug team. Together they had set up a deal for kilo quantities of heroin to be delivered to Graven late at night on the Munich to Frankfurt Super highway by a Tunisian heroin dealer. The meeting was set for an autobahn rest stop not far from the city of Wuerzburg. There was a restaurant and gas station on either side of the highway which could be accessed from either side through an underground pedestrian walk thru tunnel. There were members of the arrest team on both sides of the tunnel keeping a close surveillance on the movements of the players. The flash was made on one end of the tunnel, and then Graven, one of the state police agents and the dealer were then going to walk through the tunnel to the other side where the heroin was to be exchanged for the money. While all of this was happening some of the German agents were becoming anxious since it was taking so long for the deal party to show on the exchange side of the tunnel. Two agents then decided that they would walk through the tunnel and try to see what was holding up the deal. As they entered the tunnel, the deal team was already in the tunnel walking towards the other side. As the two groups neared each other, the Tunisian dealer apparently recognized one or more of the agents approaching them. He panicked, and pulled out a very long and sharp knife with which he began attacking the police agents he was with. He slashed the German Agent with Graven severely, and was going for Graven, slashing him badly with his knife. Graven, seeing that the German agent was critically injured and on the ground, pulled his weapon, which was one of the .380 cal pistols and fired 5 rounds into the attacking heroin dealer's torso. The Tunisian kept up his attack and had to be physically thrown to the pavement by Graven. Bad news travels quickly, and the German agents on both side of the tunnel knew that something bad was happening and they rushed into the tunnel. They arrived to find their agent and Graven bleeding badly from their knife wounds, and the Tunisian was laying on the pavement. Before an ambulance could arrive at the scene the Tunisian died from his gunshot injuries. If the weapon Graven was carrying was at least a 9mm, he would have incapacitated, or killed the slasher much sooner. At that time, I was in Stuttgart meeting with team of informants who were setting up another deal. Before I went to that meeting I had been with members of the level 2 drug team from Stuttgart, and I informed them of where I was going and with whom I was meeting. This was something I periodically did when no one else knew of my activities in any evening. This was in response to the Bad Homburg deal. Graven, after being treated at the German hospital called the Level 2 agents in Stuttgart and told them that something had occurred during the deal and he requested they contact me and tell me to come to the Wuerzburg State Police Office.

That night there was an extremely heavy fog that sat over the autobahn system between Stuttgart and Wuerzburg, and I knew the drive would be hazardous. Since it was the wee hours of the morning, and I was a bit tired I asked one of the Stuttgart agents to drive me to Wuerzburg. Most of the drive was at a maddening slow speed, and when I arrived I was pleased to see that while he had been badly wounded Graven was up, and alert, and he filled me in on the incident. After all of the formalities, Graven, and I went to his covert apartment where I made the necessary notifications to the CID Headquarters in Heidelberg, and then we tried to get a few hours sleep before heading back to our office. There was a massive investigation conducted by both the American and German Police which ultimately showed that there was adequate justification for the shooting. After all of the smoke cleared, for going to the aid of his German partner in the face of an armed adversary who was trying to kill both of them. Graven was awarded the well-deserved Soldiers Medal, which is the highest peacetime award for bravery that the Army has.

About this time things slowed down a bit. It was December, and the weather would be changing soon. It was time for a respite from all of the activities of the last year. CID Headquarters in Washington sent a request for investigation to us in Heidelberg. They had received information from a member of congress that American military firearms were being sold at a flea market in Liege which is a large city in Belgium. The congressman wanted answers, and frankly, so did we. Belgium, while not a country we were prohibited from entering, was one of the NATO countries that we were not allowed to work in covertly. The spirit of the ban was that we shouldn't covertly work drug cases. No mention was ever made about weapons trafficking. The person to whom this mission was assigned was, of course, yours truly. I selected Graven to accompany me and off we went in my shiny Opal sports model covert car. I left the German license Plates on the car so that we wouldn't draw attention to our activities. We had a nice drive up there and found some nice rooms in the Liege Holiday Inn. I decided that I would take a walkabout to see how things were laid out around the Flea Market area which we learned from the hotel desk clerk was close by. I arranged for Graven and I to meet later in the hotel bar where we would try to scare up some information about the flea market which ran for the entire weekend. When we met, Graven and I were both somewhat surprised to see some older men dressed in US Army World War 11 uniforms. Some were wearing Officer ranks and others had on enlisted men's uniforms with the ranks of Private, PFCs and some Sergeants. The big surprise with the uniforms were the decorations they wore in row after row on their jackets. The other surprise was that they all were speaking English. As we tried to figure out what was going on here I spotted a very thin Gentleman walk into the Bar. His presence was something that commanded respect. I was speechless for a short while, and then said to Graven, "Holy Shit, that's General Westmoreland". Graven was more interested in looking at some attractive females at a nearby table, and didn't even blink when I said it. he mumbled something like "Bullshit these guys are probably from a movie cast". In a former life I had worked closely with General William Westmoreland providing personal security (Read Bodyguard) for him on a few occasions when he visited Ft Bragg. One time when he was hospitalized there. At that time I spent many evening hours in conversation with him. I found him to be a very pleasant, easy to get along with man. I also experienced the dark side of him one night while he was trying to reach his deputy by phone and some young lieutenant in Washington didn't know where he was. that was a lesson I'll bet, that the Lieutenant never forgot. I know I didn't.

I decided that I was going to go over to his table where he sat alone, and renew our old aquaintance. Graven thought that I was crazy. As I approached him, he looked up but since I was sporting long hair and a beard, he just smiled and gave me a friendly nod. I broke the ice by addressing him as General Westmoreland, and told him of our previous encounters at Ft Bragg, and also in Vietnam. He invited me to join him and I did and ordered a beer. I told him that Graven and I were CID Agents and he looked at me strangely due to our appearance, and then I told him of our mission in Liege and I asked him what brought him here. He then pointed towards the men in uniform and said that he was there to attend the anniversary of the beginning of the "Battle of the Bulge" which began on 16 December 1944, the anniversary of which was tomorrow. He was joining with other members of his former WW11 unit and would be making a token march to Mons, Belgium the next morning. He said that he couldn't make the entire march due to his physical condition, but would be there for part of it. All of the others who couldn't make it would finish the march in a bus, and then join in the festivities that the Belgian government had put in place. By this time some recognition was flowing into him and he stated that he remembered me from the hospital stay. We talked for quite a while and then before we left him I asked for his autograph, which he wrote out on a napkin, which I still have to this day. I also asked him for one more autograph which I was going to bring back and show to a major assigned to the headquarters in Heidelberg. Now the Major was a complete jerk who no one, not even his wife liked. We pledged to have another beer before we left for Heidelberg in a few days, and then we left him with a growing crowd at the bar. for the next few days we wandered around the flea market which was huge. We saw a lot of WW11army equipment, and even some German and English weapons, but no American equipment. We also visited the Browning weapons factory and museum where some of our covert pistols had been made while the factory was under Nazi Germany's control.

When we returned to Heidelberg we went to the major's office and I tried to give him the autograph the General had signed, and he said Bullshit, and rolled it into a ball and threw it into the trashcan. I verbally chastised him for it and as we walked out of his office I said over my shoulder that he should pray that "Westy" doesn't come by our headquarters, because if he did I was going to drop a dime on him. A look of panic came across his face and he was last seen kneeling by the trashcan looking for the napkin.

The trip to Belgium was a welcome relief from the constant turmoil of the Level One operation but we all needed a complete break from the informants, German police and the drug traffickers with whom we had daily close contact. Roy F, the newly assigned Agent who was the successor in Munich had a brilliant idea. The Heidelberg Officer Club sponsored the

Heidelberg Ski Club which was planning a weeklong ski trip to Jugoslavia, or what is now known as Slovenia. This would be the perfect break. No stress, and phone calls in the middle of the night. Just relaxation and good skiing. We all signed up, some of the team brought wives, but no kids. We would be staying at a 4 star hotel in the town of Bled with full pension which means that all meals and drinks were included. To get us all ready for the week, and to really get to know each other, we all met on a Sunday afternoon at the local spa just north of Heidelberg which on Sundays, was completely textilefrei (no clothing allowed). Some of the American wives were a little nervous about this aspect of the trip but after about 5 minutes of complete nudity in the saunas and swimming pools, felt at ease and really enjoyed the experience. We took a large German tour bus from Heidelberg to Bled, and were pleased and surprised at the luxury of the old and very quaint hotel we were staying at. The first morning on the slopes was a beautiful sunny day. A lot of us who hadn't been skiing for a while started on the bunny slopes and gradually made it up to the mountain slopes with the help of Graf, who is an expert skier. One of the best features of the slopes we were on is that while sking down the mountain, every so often you would encounter a Slivovitz stand where you can ski up, get a shot of this flammable liquor, and continue to the next stand. A day of this makes for very happy skiers. The return to the hotel in the evening was a sight to behold. As the skiers left the bus they would race to the hotel's sauna in an attempt to thaw out the extremities. Once inside there was a constant jockeying for a good position. The sauna was larger than most you would find in a European hotel and would be filled bumper to bumper with all of the skiers. Those who were stuck with a seat in the lower area would be subject to being hit on the head by male "junk" as the latecomers scrambled over them to get to a higher location. Once settled there was a buzz of conversation about the days activities on the slopes, and it was obvious that everyone was having a great time. After the first day you could see people leaving the bus and while running for the sauna their clothing would be strewn along the path to the spa. Sometimes it worked and sometimes not. Our group was not the only one staying at this hotel, and we quickly met the other groups. That first evening in the sauna there was a notable meeting. with the sauna chamber filled with naked people we found mixed in with our group two matronly looking British school teachers who were sitting quite properly in their skirted bathing suits with the look of the horrified on their faces. They were obviously scandalized but apparently didn't want to be rude so they stayed with our crazy bunch. I swear I saw a forced smile on one of their faces. The ladies complained to the management, and received an education on sauna protocol from the owner. They did however rejoin our herd later in the week. Also later in the week there was a skirmish with the German bus driver. When he dropped us off at the slopes he was supposed to park the bus in a specific spot so that returning skiers could get into the bus and warm up. He however, would drop us off and then drive to heaven only knows and return shortly before we were to leave for the hotel. This aggravated a number of the skiers. In the middle of the week it came to a head when he parked the bus locked it and walked away. A number of us made one pass down the slopes and then decided to put up our skis and walk the short distance into the village nearby and have a beer. The driver was no where to be found so I took it on myself to find the outside door control lever and let the folks in to the bus. As we were walking away from the bus we heard the sound of a raging bull asking who had opened the door to the bus. It was the driver who was steaming. I quickly owned up to it and asked where he was and why did he lock the riders out of the bus. As this exchange was occurring we were walking towards each other with evil looks on our faces, I gave my gloves a shake much like you will see at a Bruins/Rangers game and they came flying off of my hands. Cooler heads prevailed and Graf jumped in and saved the bus driver from a horrible ass kicking. The rest of the trip was great, and just what the team needed to unwind. We pledged to do it again but never did.

To further illustrate that covert drug operations are at times very dangerous, There were other instances when the use of reliable weapons was welcomed. One such time was when we were hosting a DEA Agent on a trip from Washington, DC to Germany who was collecting intelligence on a terrorist bombing of a bar in Berlin known As the La Belle Disco Bar that was an American soldier hangout and in which several soldiers had been injured by the blast. The DEA agent was in a good position to succeed in his mission since he was a retired Army CID Agent, and a former CID Narcotics agent who many of us knew from the Vietnam war era. Now, why you ask, was the DEA interested in this terrorist attack on this soldiers hangout bar. the bar was a known drug connection and DEA had an interest in that aspect of its operation and potential connection to terrorist activities He joined us in Heidelberg and we exchanged information on the bombing and then headed out to the field to meet with other

CID agents who had been involved in the initial investigation of this terrorist attack on US personnel.

The first stop was in Nuernberg, where our agent there, known as Graf, had his hand on the pulse of drug activities in and around the city, and who had extremely good connections with the Nuernberg City KRIPO, the Bavarian State Police, and German customs officers. He was also firmly entrenched with the criminal element in the Nuernberg, and was known as a pimp with good drug connections. The drug deals .he made were always high quality. His pimp cover was established through some of his top professional informants who were in fact high class hookers who were well known in the nightclub scene. The meeting we set up coincided with one of our monthly field meetings of our agents. Which were established in order to make all of our agents familiar with areas of responsibility of the others in order to be able to move into town and assume his duties in an emergency. We met in Graf's covert apartment and held some good discussions with him. At dinner time we went to a very nice old German restaurant, and enjoyed a fine meal. The DEA agent then wanted to see what some of the night life was all about. And since CID was already working closely at the headquarters level with DEA on a fraud and drug investigation. Graf suggested that we go to a predominately black GI Hangout club where the key figure in this investigation was known to frequent. Not wanting to look like an invasion hitting the club we filtered in during a period of an hour or so, and soon took over a number of tables which were close together. We continued our discussions and few hours after our arrival, Graf said to the group that the subject of the investigation, (Mario) had just arrived. Graf then approached him and invited him to join us at our tables. He accepted and we were soon like old friends. The conversation got a little intense with him and a little friendly competition got under way when one of the group wanted a light for his cigarette (Yes, the good old days of smoking indoors) Graf, as flamboyant as he was, took a 100 German mark bill (about $30.00 US) from his pocket, lit it and passed it to the smoker who fired up his cigarette. Mario seeing this, also lit a 100 mark bill, held it for a short while, and then dropped it on the floor. Sitting in the next table from us were two men who were obviously American GIs. When they saw the competition at the next table they began to try and Catch the bills before they hit the floor and extinguish the flames. It was comical to watch this display. When they both tired of this play, things settled down at our table and I took one of Graf's hooker informants out onto the dance floor, and we began to slow dance. One of our agents was sitting at a booth directly across from the table where the main activity, and conversation was taking place. As I danced closer to him he changed position, and placing his feet on the booth seat, assumed what was a good seated firing position. I mention this since at the time he was holding his 9mm browning in that firing position, aiming at the table across the floor from him. As I got even closer I asked him what in the hell he was doing, and he replied that he was going to write a terminal CIR on that mother right now. Turning back I could see that he was aiming directly at Mario. To interpret what he said, we wrote intelligence reports known as CIRs (Criminal Intelligence Reports) on all our activities, and a terminal report dealt with the final disposition of that case. In other words, he was saying he was ready to shoot Mario. As bad a person as Mario was we didn't need this here and now.

I turned to the table, still dancing between Mario and the agent, and got the attention of one of the agents. I pointed at the preparing shooter trying to get the agents assistance in defusing this potentially serious situation. When I was finally able to do this hell started to break loose at the table where Mario was sitting. He had apparently also seen what was occurring across the dance floor and was scurrying to get away from the table.

When Mario finally broke loose he made a beeline to the bar where he planted himself on a barstool and began to whisper something to the bartender. The hairs on my neck were at attention. I walked over to Mario and began to calm him down by saying that the guy with the gun was just screwing around and didn't mean anything. I stayed with mario for about 30 minutes and in general conversation resumed what was being said earlier at the table about looking for a long term heroin connection. In the interim, Graf, seeing that something evil was approaching had called another informant of his who was a Karate instructor and a regional champion, and told him to get down to the club ASAP. The informant said that he would come and bring one of his classes with him. While things were settling down, Mario and I were planning on meeting in northern Italy the following spring, and I thought that we had talked our way out of trouble.(WRONG AGAIN), My gun wielding friend from the other end of the club could be seen walking across the dance floor directly for us with his gun out again. OH SHIT!!

The Karate class with the informant began to arrive and Graf was having the informant strategically place the class members around the club. The bartender, who was hovering closely to Mario, then reached under the bar and began to pullout what looked like a shotgun. Graf, who could always be found carrying a plastic shopping bag around with him pulled from it a sawed off shotgun which also accompanied him everywhere he went. It was the personification of a Mexican standoff. Before it turned into a meeting at the OK Corral, a signal went out to all agents to exit ASAP. On the way out someone fired a shot, which thankfully went unanswered. Back at Graf's apartment we settled down and had a few more quiet drinks. The DEA agent, who just a few years earlier had been a part of a similar group, said "you guys are crazy". The Agent who was playing Wyatt Earp in the club began prowling around the apartment which was in a very good neighborhood, and was very well maintained by a German Housekeeper. Graf picked up on it and told him that he was to stay off of the balcony and was not to pee off of it into the yard below. However, Graf neglected to include any other body function in his warning, and when he had the urge to loose his dinner, he found a stainless steel bowl in the kitchen which he began to fill, and then placed in Graf's refrigerator. No one saw this and the night progressed until everyone grabbed a soft location and crashed for the night. The next morning as Graf began to prepare breakfast for everyone he opened the refrigerator and almost had a coronary. Im sure he was heard for miles. He received a halfhearted apology, and then he banned the miscreant from ever coming to Nuernberg again.

Another notable incident that included weapons, the Karate class, and crossing into neighboring countries began in Munich at a popular disco and drug connection club. The agent that was assigned to the Munich office had been on the streets for a number of years and the toll of the job was getting to him. He was drinking heavily, and even his informants were concerned about him. This was when Gary was still with us, and we had been discussing the possibility of bringing him in from the field to a desk job. One night while preparations were being made to relocate him. He went to a high end disco and drug connection establishment. It is not known what started the incident, but he was taken forcibly from the club by some of the regulars, and beaten and robbed of his money and his assigned handgun. The informant who had been with us for quite a while called and informed another agent who he knew, of what had happened. When the information reached us we instituted what was known as the Agent Recovery Plan. This was a plan, when an agent in the field hadn't been heard from over the course of two days by anyone on the team, a call would go out to all team members to gather his best informants, and meet at the agents covert apartment, then we would notify the local police and begin a structured search for the missing agent. Thankfully, circumstances had not arisen that made us implement the plan for such a purpose. We had tested it a few times when for operational necessity we needed to get everyone together for a short notice operation. At the time that this situation presented itself, Gary and I were meeting with police and an informant about 5 hours from Munich. It was a good thing that the autobahns had no speed limits on them, because we flew across Germany to make the meeting that evening. When we arrived we quickly assessed the information and made an operational plan to go to the club and make contact with the manager, who we knew was heavily involved in drug trafficking. We would try the soft approach first and if that didn't work we would get hardnosed and put a lot of pressure on the people and the club. Graf was instructed to get the Karate bunch down

from Nuernberg for the operation. When we arrived at the club
it was early evening and no customers were present. We entered
and took separate tables covering most of the club. Gary,Graf
and I contacted the manager who claimed ignorance and was
very arrogant about it. His attitude tipped us that he knew more
than he was telling us. We told him that if the agent deserved the
beating we would understand, and here would be no problem
but on principal, we wanted the gun. If we got it back we would
leave and there would be no further trouble. The manager
challenged us and then Graf called his Karate informant over
and in the presence of the manager told him to place his class,
who were all wearing their German Karate society jackets
around the stage that held his disco equipment which had to
be worth multiple thousands of dollars, and if we gave them a
signal they would destroy all of it, and anyone who interfered.
We felt pretty sure that he wouldn't call the police because of
their heavy involvement in the wholesale drug .trade. This got
the managers attention and he gave us access to his employees
that worked in the back of the club where they witnessed the
agent being dragged out of the club, and finally got a name
and address from the manager who was visibly shaken by that
point. Graf took his karate contact and went to the address of
the man named as the force behind the attack. Graf knocked
at the door and the man answered the door wearing only a pair
of jockey shorts and an undershirt. Graf pulled from his pocket
a large switchblade knife that got the man's attention. He then
grabbed him by his privates and placed the knife to them saying
if the guy didn't answer his questions correctly he would start to
cut his privates off, taking a long time to do it. The man took
Graf at his word and told him that he and the others thought

that the drunk they pulled out of the club probably had drugs on him and they wanted them. He also told Graf where in the apartment he had hidden the pistol. Graf retrieved the gun and returned to the club where we confirmed by visual inspection of the serial number that this was the gun in question. When asked if the club manager was in on it he said that he was the one who told him and his friends about the possibility of a lot of money and drugs on the agent, and if they found them he wanted a cut. During the interim period at the club, the team was busy drinking and intimidating the customers who had started to arrive for the evening. When we were ready to leave the club we called for the drink bill which we thought would be substantial. The manager took the bill from the bartender and told us everything was on the house, and would we please never come back. Gary and I did return a few weeks later and found that a small speakeasy type door had been placed in the main entrance and patrons had to ring a doorbell to gain entrance after being screened by a doorman/bouncer. The manager came to the door, saw us and had a look or sheer panic on his face. We just said hi to him and walked away.

Things started to calm down after a while, and we all resumed a more normal life again. The Munich agent was replaced by a more stable individual and business started to pick up again. The Munich agent who disappeared after loosing his gun, had driven the next day to Heidelberg, and turned himself in to a drug and alcohol program the army had in operation. That action precluded us from speaking with him, and so we took the next action needed and that was to have his name put into a witness protection type of program wherein people who were in danger for one reason or another were relocated back to the

US incognito, and placed in a clean, untraceable assignment. Our man and his family were ready for retirement so he was placed on emergency leave until his retirement paperwork had been processed. I spoke with him by phone a few years later and found that he had been hired as a rural deputy for a sheriff's Office in California. He was happy and had readjusted to his new job. All is well that ends well.

There was a member of the level 2 drug team in Kaiserslautern who was excelling at that level of drug suppression. He was working for Paul C. from the Macdonald case in Ft Bragg who had also transferred to Germany. During a training meeting we were holding in Kaiserslautern, he expressed interest in trying out for a vacant position we had. I agreed to a trial and had him temporarily transferred to the DST office in Heidelberg. He was eager to go, but there were things that had to be done to see if he could work in our crazy world. He was brought down to Stuttgart and turned loose in an area of town that was kind rough and had more than its share of drug oriented bars and night clubs, some of which catered primarily with US black soldiers. He was given some confidential funds and told to make several drug buys of various amounts. We also sent in to the same bars, some of our informants without his knowledge. They were to maintain a watch on him and see how he handled himself and the people he was to meet and buy from. They were also an emergency alarm in case he got into a bind in any of the clubs. We also had some Kripo and CID agents close by in the event things went sour. Thus prepared, he was sent into the area where he went into 5 different bars and clubs and had no problem making contact inside, and making buys from dealers of user quantity of heroin and one buy of 50 grams of meth. At a prearranged time he met with two of the agents from my team and was removed from the area to where he was debriefed and where he turned the purchased drugs over to one of the KRIPO agents. That was step one. But, first we had another scheduled monthly meeting in the Wuerzburg area. We would introduce our new prospective agent to the rest of the team. We made the introduction, and he seemed to get along with everyone just fine. That was step 2, acceptance by the team. After the meeting we all went to the Wuerzburg festival grounds where a wine fest was underway. It was like an Octoberfest, but just with wine instead of beer. We had a good time there drinking and singing German drinking songs. I was sitting next to Graven who was our local host, and across the table was our prospect who I guess at this point, we can call Ken. He was getting a little under the weather and I was watching him closely. He had semi-glazed eyes that told me he was nearing the end of the evening's festivities. He was staring very intently at Graven, and was fingering his wine glass strangely. I could see that something unpleasant was about to happen. But, before I could say something to Graven, Ken grabbed his glass and reached across the table and struck Graven on the cheek with it cutting him slightly. I grabbed Ken and was holding him down on the table when a few others from the team jumped in and, as we hustled him out of the wine tent, I heard someone say that the police were coming. When we were far enough away from the tent we stopped and as I was getting ready to eat Ken's ass out, Ken burst into tears and said that he was sorry and didn't know what came over him. He said he was ready to take any punishment that was to be metered out. Ken grabbed Graven and gave him a manly hug, and again said that he was sorry and that he was prepared to go to jail, or have his ass whipped for assaulting a superior officer, Graven being a CW3. In a very characteristic way Graven told him that he accepted the apology and the incident was dead as of that minute. This shocked Ken, and then Graven said words that fully described the team, He told Ken that what happened in the team was team business only, and he asked me to assign Ken to him for the rest of his evaluation. I agreed, and then we went to Graven's apartment to finish out the night. After that incident Ken followed Graven around like a lost puppy. As the evaluation continued for the following weeks, Ken proved himself time and time again. He gained the respect of both the team's agents and the German police as well. His acceptance to the team was assured, and he was assigned full time as Graven's assistant in the Wuerzbuerg area. When I last saw Ken a few years ago in Tampa, he was a lieutenant running the Tampa PD drug squad, and He since has been promoted to Major on the Tampa PD. He has more than proven himself, and I am proud to have been able to help send him on his way to success.

Speaking of guns and some of the problems they cause, There was an Agent assigned to the Level 2 Drug Suppression Team in the medieval city of Bamberg where I began my drug suppression career with the legendary agent "Ace", who was a good Agent, and should have been assigned to a general crimes team and not drugs. He tried and tried to get a good drug deal put together, but just couldn't. He was too well known in Bamberg to try anything covert, and he couldn't recruit an informant to do the ground work for him.

On a Saturday night, when I was actually at home for a change, the CID Duty Agent at the Headquarters called me and related that the Drug Agent in Bamberg had been ambushed on a dark highway and shot at and nearly killed by some unknown persons. Well, that killed that weekend. I decided that I would jump in on this one. I called some Agents around the country and told them that we would be having a meeting the next morning and they should be prepared to be away from home for an unknown period of time.

I was in the office early on Monday after having met with the Agents I called on Saturday and the CID Group Operations Officer on Sunday and had briefed him on what I wanted to do. He was in favor of my plan which was to take a group of proven covert Agents and insert them into the drug scene in Bamberg, and to gather intelligence on the shooting. They were to remain covert and to pull out all of the stops and put the fear of the lord into the Bamberg criminal element. The agents had already worked out their cover stories, and so we descended on Bamberg like Atilla and his happy bunch would have done. One of the Agents was a "Large" guy who I labelled as the "Swedish mercenary" based on his appearance. He was the first of my merry men to meet resistance on the street, and after that encounter the Bamberg underground became very passive, but wouldn't, or couldn't provide the info we were looking for. We stayed in town for a week, and during that period, not an ounce of dope could be found anywhere in the city. Towards the end of the week I gathered a few of the marauders and went out to the scene of the shooting. The german police had processed the crime scene and had left chalk marks wherever they found evidence. So using what was left, we reconstructed the crime. The Agent in his statement said that he was driving on the road at about 50 MPH when a dark colored car came alongside of his car and someone in the back seat started shooting at him. He braked and the car sped away. He said that he threw himself down on the front bench seat to avoid being hit by the bullets. Before we went out to the shooting scene we inspected the car and saw that there were 8 9mm bullet holes in the right front door of the car. And there was a chalk circle about 2 feet in diameter on the street where the empty shell casings had been found by the police. We returned to the Bamberg CID office and we all locked ourselves in the conference room, and almost as if on signal we began to cuss the one person who had brought us all together. I grabbed one of the guys and we went to the office of the Special agent in charge and asked him who from the office had processed the shooting crime scene. We were told that the Bamberg KRIPO had been on the scene so no CID team went. I exploded, and then began to tell the SAC that the crime scene showed that if the cars were travelling at 50 MPH it seemed unlikely that all of the shell casings would be found in a 2 foot circle, and the bullet holes in the car could be so symmetrical and tightly grouped. His chin dropped about a foot and he began to use the same cuss words that we had used in the conference room. I took the SAC and we corralled the shooting victim in an empty office and just barely started on him when he began to break down and cry, and told us that he did the shooting himself in order to get some attention from higher ups on the out of control drug scene in Bamberg. Well, some good came from it all, We had dried up the drug flow for a while in the city which made the KRIPO very happy and it also caused their informants to pursue different drug sources. The upheaval brought some dealers who they hadn't known about to the surface and gave them new targets. The Agent was removed from Bamberg and reassigned to the Heidelberg office while the higher ups decided what to do about him. During this period it was discovered that he was suffering from some exotic disease that could only be treated at Walter Reed Hospital in Washington, DC. It was felt that disciplinary action would serve no purpose, and he was transferred to Walter Reed for treatment.

.In the circles we traveled, we met all sorts of people, both good and some very bad. It was during this time period that terrorist gangs were running rampant and their targets were often American Generals, and US military bases. The headquarters of the US Army in Europe was in Heidelberg, and even with Military Police guarding the facility it came under attack from the Bader-Meinhof Gang which eventually changed its name to the Red Army Fraction (RAF). They infiltrated the base in stolen vehicles, and planted bombs hidden in propane tanks near the Officers Club which killed a number of US and German personnel. The bombs were homemade, using the propane bottles filled with a PETN explosive known as Flex-X. This was the same type of explosive that was used in several other murderous bombings throughout Europe. Also stolen by RAF terrorists, and US Forces personnel were CAL .45, AND .22 Cal target pistols used by the US pistol shooting team. There were also M-26 fragmentation hand grenades, which suited the terrorist very well. Another terrorist who was very busy in the area was the one known as "The Jackal", whose real name was Illyich Rameriz Sanchez, a South American born stone killer, who held no remorse for all of the killings he was responsible for. He acquired both Cal .45 pistols and an unknown number of the hand grenades stolen from US ammunition storage facilities in Germany. On one occasion he used the stolen grenades in an attack on a Paris business known as the Drug Store killing several people. The .cal .22 pistols were also used in killings by members of the RAF. There were also roadside bombs set by the RAF in Germany, and also in an attempt on the life of Gen Alexander Haig who was traveling in Belgium with a full security team of highly trained CID Agents. It became clear that whoever Had stolen the explosives and guns had access to high security areas. I was faced with something that I knew was going to make me unpopular with a lot of people. I approached the CID Commander and told him of my plan which would have to be approved at the 4 Star General level in Heidelberg. The CID Commander accompanied me to this high level meeting, and I laid the plan out. It was simple but would not be accepted easily by the rest of the Americans in Germany. I called for a 100% inventory of all Flex X explosives from every storage area in Europe. Looking for a lot number that was found in an unexploded bomb left behind by the RAF. I also wanted a search for any place that the lot number of the hand grenades had been shipped for the past 5 years, and all weapons storage areas where the stolen pistols had been would be completely inventoried to see what, if anything else, was missing. This would make commanders all over Europe steam. It took almost 6 months for every location to provide the wanted data, but what it showed was that there were US forces personnel, both military and civilians, and German employees who were involved in the thefts of the weapons and explosives, and that the stolen goods were then funneled into a location where they were then handed out from this common source to the various terrorist groups for use in their terror campaigns.

A number of people were identified as being involved with this operation several of which were active duty soldiers from the Hanau, Germany area. The continent wide search also told us the approx. amount of explosives and guns which were still in the hands of the terrorists. There were some commanders who balked at this tasking, and two who refused. They were taken care of in short order by the 4 star in Heidelberg who relieved them on the spot.

Other contacts we had with the terrorists were more in keeping with our mission. There was one of the hierarchy of the RAF, who with his girlfriend, wanted to make a transaction with the drug world. He wanted to trade drugs for explosives and weapons. This would be a tricky operation since the RAF people had been trained by the Russian KGB, and would be on the sharp lookout for any signs of police action in this operation. Several meetings were held with this character, and as he was driving with his girlfriend to a meeting where samples would be shown from both ends of the deal there was a very bad wreck on the highway that killed both of them. The terrorist, Henning Beer, had some high grade heroin on him when he crashed.

During another monthly meeting we received a call from the chief of the Baden Wuerttemburg State Police (LKA) drug team. He had a deal which had been set up weeks earlier for 2 kilos of heroin that was to be delivered to an American buyer. The dealer had called his LKA contact, and told him that the heroin was in town and he wanted to meet with the American buyer to see the money and then the transfer would take place. The location for the flash was set for a restaurant which was way out in the country. It was more than 20 miles from the city of Karlsruhe. The surveillance and arrest team was headed there at that time and would be in place well before the buy team arrived. Since the gang was all together I said that we would be there in force. We met with a couple of the LKA team in Mannheim and followed them to a very nice restaurant which was on the French border. I could just see what was about to happen. We would end up in France and get caught by the French police who we learned earlier were not eager to have the German police on their side of the border. There was a strong turf jealousy that had been established years before when a shooting occurred during a deal. Oh well, another adventure loomed. At the restaurant we met the Turkish dealer, who had 3 others with him. We had the owner set up a large table, and ordered a meal while starting to work the deal. The Turks were not very tuned in to their Muslim faith and several bottles of wine were brought to accompany the meal, which by the way was fantastic German country cooking. There were several other parties at the restaurant including one which was made up of male and female members of the LKA surveillance team which we had met earlier on the way out to the restaurant, and received the flash of 150,000 German Marks. While we talked business with the Turkish group it was decided that after the flash, the money would stay with my team, until the older dealer who was obviously in charge of this deal, and I went to another, as yet undisclosed location to get the heroin. I would then call the restaurant telling the group here that I had the goods, give them a code word, and then they would give the money to the turks who remained behind. To add to this developing adventure the Turks were shown the guns we had and told if anything happened to me they would all be shot. To make it sweeter, they showed us the guns they were carrying and everyone had a good laugh over it. The scene was made better since the Turks were starting to feel the wine we were consuming during dinner. All this occurred under the watchful eyes of the LKA team which switched out with another fresh group just before I left with the old man to get the heroin.

We drove in my car, the Red sporty Opel GTE. That really made a good impression on the Turk. The LKA Informant had learned that the heroin was stashed in a luggage locker in a small train station just outside of Karlsruhe. The prearranged signal that was to be given when I received the drugs was that I was to scratch my left ear and then the arrest team would swoop down and arrest both of us. At the same time, the second arrest team which would be notified by radio at the restaurant would make the arrest there of the Turks who had stayed behind. As we approached the train station I began looking for the Arrest team which was to be in place. This was more of a private game with me, trying to identify the very professional surveillance group. We walked into the station and the dealer produced a key and opened one of the lockers and pulled out a large plastic shopping bag which I opened while it was still somewhat hidden in the locker, and saw that inside there were two smaller bags, each about the size of a small box of sugar. Using my ever present switchblade knife I punctured one bag and took a small sample of the powder out and gave it a quick tongue test. BINGO!! As I put my knife away I reached and scratched my left ear, and NOTHING HAPPENED!!. My mind jumped back to the fiasco in Nuernberg all those years ago. As I reached for my gun to make an illegal arrest, we were jumped by a group of men who looked like train station janitors, complete with brooms. One of them smacked me on the head and I saw stars. We were both handcuffed and then separated, with the Turk being hustled out of the station, while I was knocked to the ground. Once he was outside, others, who I recognized as LKA agents joined us at the locker, secured the heroin, and then began to have a jolly time laughing. The idea, which was never passed to me, was that they wanted to make a big production about the arrest, and then use it as an interrogation technique on the Turk later telling him that I had given the LKA all of the information on the deal, thereby keeping the real informant confidential, and available for other deals with the same Turkish bunch. They didn't want to tell me earlier about this so that the arrest would look authentic. That sort of thing was brought to a screaming halt right then. The LKA was very apologetic and they even paid for the post deal drinks back at the restaurant. Lucky for them, my guys didn't make any smart ass remarks about it, although I could see smirks going around the table.

Later I heard that the arrest went smoothly at the restaurant, with the armed Turks there being overwhelmed by the LKA team.

My tour of duty in Germany, which had lasted for an unprecedented 7 years of extensions was coming to a close. Graven, was the predictable successor to take the Team. He ran it well for a number of years and then became caught up in the withdrawal of US forces from Germany. With most of the combat troops being transferred, there was no longer justification for the team's mission.

I returned to Germany from Ft Hood, Texas having been sent to Texas from Heidelberg, as a replacement for a senior Warrant Officer who was retiring. I felt it was close to my retirement time and I informed the Commander there of my plans. He then sent me to Ft Sam Houston in San Antonio, Texas to monitor an investigative team which came from the CID HQs in Washington, to work a sensitive case who he felt were straying from their mission target. The case involved the Olympic Pentathlon team which was made up primarily of soldiers who were accomplished horse riders, and shooters. The Pentathlon team traveled all over the world in competition matches in preparation for the next Olympic games. There was fraud galore in the acquisition of show horses from local auctions, and donations for tax purposes where someone in collusion with the Army team would bring in a horse which was ready to keel over, and get a donation certificate for up to $500,000. Which the previous owners would then write off on their taxes, giving a sizeable kickback to the person(s) receiving the horse at Ft Hood. That person would then evaluate the horse, and reject it for some cooked up reason that made it unfit for competition. Or, take in a highly trained horse, who had championship level potential, and downgrade the value and then send the horse to an auction house where a prearranged deal would be made for someone to buy that horse. There were also allegations of travel fraud, drug use, and widespread sexual activities among the team members including both enlisted members, and Officers. This is strictly forbidden by the Army. The CID HQs team was brought back on track easily enough, and since I was wanted back in Hamburg for some trials in German court, I felt it was time to hang up my guns, and find meaningful work. I returned to Germany and after testifying at the trials of the two Turks arrested earlier, I obtained a job with the Army's Chief of Police in Europe as a Physical Security investigator for all of the then existent Nuclear Weapons storage and deployment areas within NATO, including Germany, Italy, Holland, England, Turkey, and Greece. All of which have since been closed down and the Nukes removed. While in Germany I visited with old colleagues in Stuttgart who told me of a deal that went bad resulting in the shooting death of one of the covert LKA Agents. One thing you learn when a friend and law enforcement colleague is killed in this manner is you have to learn from it and not dwell on it.

The NATO job was great, plenty of travel, and I, being the only male investigator who was not married, volunteered to take all of the out of country trips. This made everyone happy since the out of country trips were from one to 3 weeks in length and the married guys wanted to stay with their families in the Heidelberg/ Mannheim, Germany areas. The hotels I stayed at had all been reconned by earlier teams and were outstanding and had great restaurants. The only trip that I really didn't enjoy was the trip to Turkey, which was done in the company of the team from the Inspector General of Europe from Heidelberg. . I kept looking over my shoulder for someone I might have had drug business with in Germany. That and the primitive conditions we encountered made it difficult to enjoy the otherwise great scenery. During one large inspection of the largest of the Turkish nuke sites, we were observing the Turkish Army performing a vehicular movement of a nuke weapon, along with all of the required security that would be involved in an actual movement. While waiting for the convoy of vehicles to begin the road trip, a fire extinguisher went off in the target truck. As some of the Turkish soldiers rushed to see what had happened. A Turkish lieutenant stuck his head out of the back of the truck, and said that he had accidently set the extinguisher off. A Turkish Major then pulled the Lt out of the truck, pulled his cal .45 pistol from its holster, and struck the Lt across the head several times. He was then hustled out of the area, bleeding from the head wounds, and was never seen by the inspection team again. We were later informed that the whipping had been for the embarrassment he had caused to the base commander.

The other trips were much more enjoyable with the 3 week trip through Italy being the best. All of the Italian base Commanders were in competition with each other over who would be the best host. Elaborate luncheons were held and the local wines were in plentiful supply. This of course was after the inspections were over, and there could be no suspicion of favoritism on the part of the inspection team. This was also found to be the case at the various bases in Greece. While on my last trip to Italy, I was driving in a rented Mercedes, sporting a full beard and my long hair from the drug days, from the Pisa area to the HQs Installation in Vicenza in the northern part of the country near Venice. When I was about half way between Verona and Vicenza I encountered a Carabinieri roadblock along a very dark stretch of the highway. when I was stopped, the Italian paramilitary police surrounded my car with their submachine guns trained on me. Since this wasn't my first rodeo, I knew something was up, and I kept my hands on the steering wheel in very plain sight. There was one of the officers who spoke very passable English and he told me to get out of the car. They still kept me under their weapons, and began a thorough search of my car. When satisfied that I didn't have what they wanted, they let me proceed. About 20 mInutes later I was pulled over by Carabinieri patrol cars that were filled with uniformed officers who also had machine guns. This was getting habit forming. After the second search I made it to the Army Base in Vicenza where I located Dan W. an old friend of mine from Germany who was stationed with the local Army CID Office. When I told him what had happened to me he told me that just hours earlier General Dozier, had been kidnapped from his living quarters in Verona by some Red Brigade terrorists and that the Italian police were out in force looking for him. That stopped my driving for the night. I hitched a ride with Dan to my hotel where I stayed until the next day. There is more to this story, but that's for another day.

I stayed with that job with NATO for a year and then was transferred to the Naval Post Graduate School in Monterey, California as a personal security Investigator with the Dept of Defense Investigative Service. There I continued my law enforcement career until I was recruited by two other friends from CID, Al P. and Col Bill P from Tucson, Az, to work at the Arizona State Law Enforcement Intelligence Agency as a supervisory Intelligence Agent in charge of the State's Organized Crime Division. This was an eye opener. I jumped at it, and after an interview with some of the Dept heads began my AZPOST certified Arizona law enforcement career. I was at first partnered with a man who was a walking encyclopedia of organized crime from the beginning of the American Mafia, to the present day, and following his promotion to manage an intelligence district, I assumed his position which brought me to investigative positions in the office of the Attorney General and then full circle to Ft Huachuca, a quiet Army Intelligence training Post in the southern part of the state, in fact just 7 or so miles from Mexico, where I was selected as the Chief of police for the installation, and acquired a Detectives commission with the Cochise County Sheriff's Office where I ended my Law Enforcement career running the Cold Case Section of the Sheriff's Office. I was at Ft Huachuca when the terrorist attacks occurred on 9/11/01 and I quickly formed the first Arizona Law Enforcement Intelligence Fusion Group which is still in operation today. This group of professionals came from all corners of Arizona, as well as the Los Angeles Police Dept. Anti-Terrorist Division (ATD), the San Diego Sheriff's Intelligence Bureau, The Intelligence Div. of the RCMP, and many more agencies who were, and still are, devoted to the protection of their areas of responsibilities.

170

Author as undercover CID Agent dealing with International Drug smugglers.

A coke spoon seized during a drug arrest in Germany

EPILOGUE

You might say that my law enforcement career was built around me being in the wrong place at the right time, or the right place at the right time depending on your perspective. I have had the pleasure of serving alongside some of the best in the business in cases of general crimes, including homicides, Criminal Intelligence, war crimes, and the full gamut of human transgressions as well as drug suppression. I have worked, and studied along with detectives who have taught me more "Stuff" than I can catalog here. I have never had an assignment where I didn't learn something that would help me in some way. I just hope that those to whom I have tried to pass on my "Stuff" can find some direction from what I have offered to them. I don't put myself up to be some sort of a super cop. In all of my investigative activities, I didn't do anything that most hard working detectives wouldn't do. It's just that I had perhaps more opportunity to be involved in those cases I have described and have had the resources to carry my investigations to a successful conclusion. Not many homicide investigators have the ability to go to the Armed Forces Institute of Pathology, one of the world's foremost authorities in human deaths of all categories, and then have the opportunity to work with the Maryland Medical Examiner who has written volumes on homicide investigations, and to have the opportunity to brain drain him about aspects of a murder case that had national attention. That plus a prosecution team that was heart and soul involved with the successful completion of the case in question. Another man who I met and made good friends with was Joe McGuiness who researched and authored the book, and movie "Fatal Vision", which is by far, the best and most accurate of any I have encountered in regards to this infamous, multiple murder case. Unfortunately Joe passed away recently, and he and his counsel will be sorely missed. After the horrible events of 9/11 I volunteered for a position as the Force Protection Program Manager (The anti/counter-terrorism program manager) for the support command of all of southern Germany, where I supervised the AT/FP operation at all of the installations, and US Army recreation hotels which were being phased out. It was a shame to see all of the historic buildings being closed and shuttered, but it was an exciting time, and in the company of another former SF trooper Marc P. We accomplished the mission. When I returned to Ft Huachuca I realized that I had experienced as much or more than most of my peers and was still able to walk. That signaled to me that it was time to retire, and I did, leaving myself with an Arizona law enforcement officer certification which I again used with the Cochise County Sheriff's Office running the Cold Case Squad for a few years. After that success I finally retired to my home in Arizona and at present have the tremendous responsibility of supervising my two tiny dogs, Dudley Winston, his baby sister Isabella. And I also salute my lovely wife Elisa who stays with me even after numerous visits from most, if not all of the strange characters written about on these pages. And, a fine retirement it is. It is to these fine Agents and their wives that I fondly dedicate this book. And, Gary Lowell Price; you are with us always. Save a cloud for me..

FIN

Printed in the United States
By Bookmasters